INSPIRed Parenting

Barbara Maddigan, M.D., FRCPC

Copyright © Dr. Barbara A. Maddigan, 2010

All rights reserved.
No reproduction in whole or in part without the written consent of the author.

Publisher: Barbara A. Maddigan
Editor: Kristann Templeton
Graphic Design: Leigh-Ann Payne
Cover Art: Monika and Timothy Noble

ISBN: 978-0-9867711-0-1
First Edition

Printed in the United States

Library and Archives Canada Cataloguing in Publication

Maddigan, Barbara, 1965-
Inspired parenting / Barbara Maddigan.

ISBN 978-0-9867711-0-1

1. Parenting. 2. Child rearing. I. Title.

HQ769.M33 2010   649'.1   C2011-900325-2

What Readers Are Saying

"I found the book informative and easy to read. Even though as a colleague I talk this talk on a daily basis as well, interestingly enough, I found myself reading it as a parent and partner and it reminded me that we don't always do as good a job with communication, in particular, in our private lives as we do in our professional lives.

I think this book would appeal to those parents who are trying to juggle the myriad demands of career, family, school and extracurricular activities, personal relationships, etc. in today's complicated world. It offers helpful advice with humor and without being judgmental, acknowledging that as parents, we are all trying to do our best, as are our kids!"
Christine Snelgrove, MD, FRCPC

"When Barbara asked me if I would read her manuscript, my first instinct was to try and find a plausible reason to say no so that I wouldn't upset her! I couldn't come up with a reason and so I read every word! To say the least I was pleasantly surprised. What could easily have been a very dry book, turned out to be as entertaining as the subject would permit. This is because Barbara writes as she speaks. I would certainly recommend that any parent read it."
David Baker, father and grandparent

"Intelligently written by a Child Psychiatrist with the experience of being a parent. Wonderfully presented from the heart in an easy-to-read and common sense format. It is a must read for everyone from the neophyte to the seasoned parent of a teenager."
Mary Wall, MD

"……a warm, thought-provoking guide to bringing out the best in our children and in ourselves as parents."
Susan Drodge, mother of 2

Inspired Parenting

As a child and adolescent psychiatrist, with two children of my own, I have had the wonderful opportunity of working with and being with great kids most of my days! Through the course of my practice and in my day-to-day life, recurrent themes have appeared to me as essential to the process of parenting and the challenges parents and families face. There is often a subtleness about parenting that is sometimes hard to master. The connection between family members is instrumental to the success of their relationship. In my clinical practice I see many of these struggles, but it is impossible to cover everything in the office setting, especially when people are in any type of medical crisis. I hope that this book will help parents and caregivers see some of these issues in a new light, which will enhance their relationships at home and the health of their children.

Raising my own children with care and, hopefully, competency is my biggest mission in life. If you're taking the time and effort to read this book, obviously you are also very interested in your family and children! Our families now are often a combination of grandparents, aunts and uncles, and family friends, all intermingled in raising our children. Many families are now either single parent or blended families, and so parents and caregivers don't always have the traditional "spouse" to confer with or to tag-team with. This is where our support team comes in; it may have many faces that change from time to time, and sometimes it may just be our own 'inner self' we talk to. That conversation is often the most useful and often the most needed.

Inspired Parenting

This book is for anyone interested in a healthy, rewarding relationship with the children in their lives! This book is also written for male and female parental figures. Men and women often have differences in their parenting style, which is important for our children, but the fundamentals of respect, communication, and other key issues in parenting are important to all of us raising children. No matter how old your child is, it is never too early or too late to self-reflect and evolve in our parenting approach! Writing this book has allowed me to reflect on my own parenting practices and has increased my own self-awareness.

"Every morning is an open door to a new world."
Leigh Hodges

Disclaimer

Please be informed that the advice and information presented in *Inspired Parenting* is not intended to replace the advice of your physician or other qualified health care professional. Before starting any new treatment, exercise program, or dietary change, please check with your physician. Should you have any health care concerns regarding yourself or your child, please consult with your physician or qualified health care professional.

Dedication

....

I dedicate this book to my parents, Marion and James Francis [Frank] Maddigan. My Mom was always full of fun and vitality - loving, inspirational and always supportive. We lost our Mom way too early, in 1999, after a heroic battle with cancer. I miss her every day, and I aspire to be like her always. She more than anyone else in my life showed me how to be the person and mother I am today. Thank you Mom. My father is a pillar, a truly amazing support, both my right and left arms! His unrelenting patience and love is always a motivation for me, his tolerance of all and everyone, inspiring. Thanks for your daily support and help Dad! I love you more than I can say. Your insight into today's issues with parenting and Monika and Timothy are amazing. Thanks for all the fantastic story telling; Monika and Timothy will remember them forever. You are an instrumental part of their lives, they love you dearly.

And I would also be lost without the never-ending love and support of my sister, Suzanne. She is appointed as my children's "second mother" by both my children and me! She is a gentle flower, always loving, always there. Thank you, Suzanne, you are a courageous soldier, dressed as a rose! I am also forever grateful to my brother, John, for his ongoing support and inspiration to think big, to believe in myself. I truly feel well-loved by my big brother! Thank you, John; it's great to be so close! I have two other wonderful sisters, Donna and Catherine, mothers themselves, who have been paving the curvy road of parenting right before my eyes. Their dedication and fortitude are inspiring. Both Catherine and Donna had special roles in my life. My eldest sister, Catherine, was often 'in charge', thus dragging me along wherever she went!

And Donna is the closest in age, and thus was often stuck with me. Being the youngest had many pearls, especially when tagging along or visiting siblings around the world. They were instrumental to my upbringing and experiences. My brother and sisters have certainly been my village. I share this not just to acknowledge their great contributions to my life, but to also illustrate how important family is. The sibling relationship is very important, very strong, and influential.

Monika and Timothy, my two children, are a daily inspiration. Through their love and support, I can strive to be my best parenting self. Kerry, my husband, has been a wonderful example of strength and understanding. Kerry, Monika and Timothy have been incredibly supportive throughout the writing of this book, for which I am truly grateful. I have been granted amazing people in my life for guidance and support.

I hope this book provides some inspiration for you to be your best inner parent. Happy reading and happy parenting!

> *"Love and trust are the best ways to make friendship grow"*
> *Anonymous*

Table of Contents

Introduction

Chapter 1:	Be Healthy, Have Fun!	5
Chapter 2:	Lessons from My Mentors	27
Chapter 3:	Kindness and Other Things Undervalued!	34
Chapter 4:	Respect	43
Chapter 5:	Being Present and Showing Up	54
Chapter 6:	Communication	61
Chapter 7:	Unplug Your Kids	72
Chapter 8:	When Your Child Is Not Succeeding	82
Chapter 9:	If I Were Principal for a Day!!	95
Chapter 10:	ADHD: The Child Who Just Can't PAY ATTENTION!	105
Chapter 11:	Anxiety and Depression: Our Worried and Sad Children	114
Chapter 12:	Humour: Laughter Really Is the Best Medicine	125
Chapter 13:	Stamina	131
Chapter 14:	Parental Praise	139
Chapter 15:	Adjusting Our Parenting Approach on an As-Needed Basis!!	143
Chapter 16:	If You Could See Me Now!	153
Chapter 17:	Words from the Peanut Gallery	161

Gratitude

Introduction

Raising my children, being a part of their lives, is incredibly rewarding, but unfortunately a time limited process - they are ours for such a short time. If we live to be 90 years old, 12-18 years of intense parenting is really only a short blip. Children are incredibly inspiring. Working with children and adolescents and their families is very gratifying and educational! I learn many things from my patients every day. My clinical practice and my own two amazing children have inspired me to write this book.

We as parents need to be healthy, relaxed, and yet focused on what is really important. Parenting can be intense, demanding, and exhausting, but mostly it should be fun and rewarding. We don't have perfect lives or perfect children. We need to accept our children for who they are, to help them reach their potential and to recognize and address what needs to change. I learn from my children every day; they have so much to teach us, we need only to listen. When I see good results from our parenting, it is so rewarding! When I see something our children are mirroring in us that I don't like, it opens my eyes even further! Children truly learn what they live; we are their most significant role models! They take on our body language, our habits, attitudes and behaviours, so we must be fully aware of this. I have dedicated a chapter on this issue as I feel it is vital information.

A healthy parent fosters a healthy marriage/family and healthy children. All children deserve love and respect and to be fully understood. It is in really understanding our children, realizing the role we play in their development, and truly accepting them for who they are, that we can maximize their potential for happiness and success, and thus our own. As parents, we need to invest our time and energy into parenting and being a healthy family and individual. I have had great conversations with friends - some are parents themselves, some are not - about parenting, goals for our children, impacts our society has on them, and countless other topics relevant to family life and parenting. These conversations have proven to be invaluable to me. Collaboration with family and friends is vital to our own self-reflection on these issues and making goals for ourselves and our children.

Check in with your spouse and children. Communication is vital. We can spend days with someone but not really talk with them. Ask your children and spouse, 'How are things going?' 'Do things need to change?' 'What's going well, and what could be better?' It helps me tremendously to do this with my children. It can be very eye opening and, even if there are no big revelations, they know you are interested and listening. Respect is vital to any relationship, especially the one with your children. Children can intuitively know if they are respected, and it will greatly influence how they interact with you. I will also spend more time on this very important issue.

Personal growth and good health are necessary to being a strong, effective, and emotionally available parent. Balancing all of this is not easy, but not impossible. Usually it is our own negative thinking that gets in the way, not our children or responsibilities. We have to think outside the box, be creative with ourselves and our children. I'll spend some time talking about our own needs as parents and our responsibility to self-care as a piece of the whole parenting puzzle!

Communication is central to relationships - the words we choose, our body language, our tone, and timing! I have a particular interest

Introduction

in communication skills in physicians. In fact, I work with a great group of physicians at Memorial University of Newfoundland and Labrador in Post-Graduate Program Development on this very important skill. Communication is a skill that can be taught and learned; some are naturally better at it than others, some need a little work! So pay attention to your communication style. Being a good listener is the first step in communicating. Studies have shown that some physicians often only give their patients 30 seconds to speak freely before they interrupt them! How is your timing? Listening to our children and partner is vital in getting the rest of the conversation right! I'll review some communication tips later.

We never arrive anywhere without help and influence. I have been blessed with incredible people in my life. My parents were and continue to be the most amazing people I have met - so caring, patient, loving, and very encouraging. More than anyone or anything, they taught me about loving my children unconditionally, in the true sense, and respecting each other and ourselves. They also taught me to be flexible and open-minded and to not take myself too seriously. These lessons have taught me so much and continue to be invaluable tools in my life.

I also have some amazing friends in my life, and I have learned much from these individuals, both personally and professionally. People come into our lives and bless us with their knowledge and wisdom. Life is to share and enjoy together; we learn so much from each other. Each one of us has something special to give, especially our children. I embrace mine and learn from them every day! Thank you Monika and Timothy!

My hope is that by sharing with you my clinical experience and knowledge, combined with my own parenting experience, that your own personal, family, and children's health will benefit. Parenting is about caring, paying attention, and having fun. Trusting our instincts is key. Most of what we read in any self-help book we really already intuitively know - we usually just need some encouragement to listen to ourselves. I hope this book gives you the confidence to listen to what you know inside of you, and to take the chances to make good, thoughtful decisions, even if they are the tough ones! Everyone makes the best decision they can, given their circumstances, knowledge, and opportunities available to them at the time. Don't be judgmental of yourself or your children; just do your best to be informed, and to maximize your potential and opportunities. By doing this you will provide great experiences for you and your family. Happy reading!

"Like children we live in a world of trust. What we have we received as a gift."
Richard J. Foster

Chapter One

....

Be Healthy, Have Fun!

....

We hear it all the time, "You need to take care of yourself." But do we REALLY listen? For most parents, the answer is, "probably not". It is really hard to be energetic, mindful, creative, caring, patient or anything else very positive when we are tired, in pain, forgetful, or unwell. Parenting is not for the weak at...anything! We can't give much to anyone when we are running on empty. Being tired or unwell can make us cranky and impatient, which does not mix well with trying to get homework done or supper prepared, or just about anything, especially tasks which require interaction with others. Unfortunately this fatigue or unwellness tends to lead to deterioration in our manners, tolerance, and overall behaviour with our own family members. Combine this with feeling cranky because we are strung out, and watch the fireworks! Of course we then usually feel guilty for losing it with the kids or with our partner in front of the kids. Then we give in to the request or behaviour we were just complaining about! Not effective, not fun, and not rewarding!

Take Control

Our behaviour is always much calmer, more predictable, and effective when we feel calm and unstressed. We feel calmer and more relaxed when we feel well physically. Our health is something we usually take for granted until something starts to fail or maybe when a friend or family member becomes ill. We need to be very proactive with our health rather than waiting until something goes wrong, which then takes way more time to fix. As we get a little older - and how fast does that happen - we start seeing subtle changes. We can't stay up really late anymore and then work all day, exercise possibly doesn't have the same immediate effect anymore, or we are more moody and so on. When children are younger, so are we. As parents of young children, we are exhausted with the demands of intense parenting! Years ago I was told of the demands of parenting, "The days are long, but the years are short". It is a powerful statement that has stayed with me.

So very quickly we can find ourselves with a little more time on our hands and, with any spare moment, we should EXERCISE! Not to be fanatical, but a little bit a day can help tremendously. I tell my patients that the magic pill does exist, in the form of physical activity! Regular moderate exercise is extremely effective in regulating our mood and in helping us deal more effectively with stress. Exercise gives us energy and protects us from many illnesses. As parents we absolutely need to be role-modeling a healthy, balanced approach to exercise for our children. It is not very effective to tell your children to get off the couch and get outside to exercise when your fingerprints are embedded into the remote control! Always remember, we lead by example. In my clinical practice I speak to most children and their families about exercise. Most often, if parents are not physically active, their children are unlikely to be. It is very difficult to instruct a child to get out for a walk every day, when they would be the only one in the household to do so. So, get up, and get moving; it is the best way to help your children develop a healthy lifestyle regarding physical activity.

Chapter One • Be Healthy, Have Fun!

Be Proactive

Health care now is much more of a collaborative approach between patients and physicians, and it is important to be very involved with your own health care. No one else knows your body better than you. If something is not right, dive in and get to the bottom of it. If you don't agree with a diagnosis or management plan, be open with your doctor about your concerns and agree on another approach. Just because you are now forty-something, or whatever age you are, doesn't mean you should be tired at 7:00 pm. Unfortunately "ageism", or blaming symptoms on our age, can start very early. For example, many women can be very sensitive to hormonal fluctuations, and hormones can start declining much earlier than we realize. If you feel something is not right, if something is changing and not for the best, investigate! Many of us are very passive when it comes to discussing things, especially very intimate issues, with our physicians. Sometimes bringing in a list of questions can be helpful, as our agenda for the appointment may get derailed by the doctor's agenda! Even as a physician I can get intimidated by the "system" as a patient. We need to not only be the best advocate we can be for our children, but also for ourselves - no one else can or will be! We are all grown up now - a staggering thought!

There are now so many options available to us to help keep ourselves well. Along with preventative healthcare, including many early detection diagnostic studies, blood work, and physical exams, we also have more and more naturopathic clinicians. Acupuncture, massage, homeopathic remedies, healing touch and yoga, to name a few, are very available to us. I once did a study comparing children with attention deficit hyperactivity disorder (ADHD) taking traditional treatments alone versus traditional treatment with either massage or yoga. The groups of children taking their regular treatment with either massage or yoga did better than the group on traditional treatment alone! (Maddigan, B et al, The Effects of Massage Therapy and Exercise Therapy on Children/Adolescents with Attention Deficit Hyperactivity Disorder, The Canadian Child and Adolescent Psychiatry Review, Mar. 2003 (12):2). Our brains are complex and can respond to many interventions. We have to find the correct combination for ourselves.

I speak from personal experience when advocating for our own health and well-being. I started yoga with my current teacher nine years ago and it changed my life. I vividly remember thinking at 45 minutes into my first one and a half hour class that yoga would make a great corporal punishment for criminals! But I made it through the session and didn't miss a class for three solid years. I still attend Barbara's classes and practice every day! Yoga gave me back my confidence in my body's strength. Barbara has been truly inspirational - she helped me get my life back! I'm sure you will enjoy her interview in the next chapter. I also remember feeling amazed when I drove home from yoga at 9:15 pm that there were so many people still awake and up and about! My life had become very home-based. I was the Queen of, "I don't have time for yoga". That perspective did nothing for me.

Drop The Excuses!

Being too busy is such a common default for many of us; it's safe and noble. We would really take care of ourselves if we had time, but we don't, so it's not our fault! Wow, are we good at rationalization! It is really a matter of priorities, isn't it? How can one of us with kids, a job, family, etc. have time and another one of us does not have time? We both have 24 hours to work with; we HAVE TO MAKE THE TIME!! We are in control and need to

Chapter One • Be Healthy, Have Fun!

realize we ARE the masters of our own destiny! A teacher once told me, "Barbara, the key to success is organization!" I still recall that statement many, many times! It was during my first year of full clinical training, a time of many demands, many anxieties. That advice is still helpful to me today!

In order to be organized, we need to organize our 24 hours. We can't be perfect, but we can usually accomplish our priorities. So make taking care of yourself a priority!! Nobody else will. We don't get brownie points for always putting others first! There are things of course that need absolute attention and priorization, but apart from the absolute necessities, our 20-minute walk should at least be able to compete with the dishes, vacuuming, answering the 10 telephone calls for our teenage son, or packing a lunch for our partner (does anyone do that anymore?). Our tombstone will not be inscribed, "She always had the kitchen looking so good!" and, if it did, who would care? When my children were a couple of years younger and usually in bed by 8:00 pm, I would tuck them in and then go for a walk. I didn't feel guilty about not being with them, I got the exercise I needed, and it was a great stress reliever. Now, it's hard to stay up past their bedtime! Anyone who knows me knows not to call me after 8:30 pm! So now I get some guilt-free exercise time earlier in the morning, before the children get up! I still try to exercise at times that don't interfere with family time, but sometimes, just sometimes, I need to put me first, and that's okay too! My children prefer that I am relaxed and happy, not cranky and frustrated!

Walking, what a wonderful, great way to get some exercise. Free, easy, and usually low risk of injury! A walk is good for the body and mind. Frustrations usually melt away, the mind becomes clear and so much better able to face the challenges of the day or night. The body becomes stronger, more agile, and usually lighter, with a regular dedication to the activity. Weight control, appetite control, anger control, wow, all that from a little walk. An activity we learn from a very young age at our finger tips, or rather toe tips! Once you start, it becomes very reinforcing, because your mind and body will likely love it! Start slow, short walks, and build up your time and pace. Get in short walks when you cannot go for longer ones, they all add up. Park far from the door, walk around your neighborhood for errands when able, walk to work, or maybe half-way to work. Take the stairs instead of the elevator. Get that body moving, and it will thank you in many ways - more energy, more patience, better lung capacity, and endurance. Better confidence, physical and mental, will be yours. A short walk, a few sit-ups, sensible eating, and a little chat with a friend will give you energy and balance, wonderful ingredients for calm, insightful parenting! ALWAYS remember to check with your doctor before starting a new exercise program! Be smart, be safe (walk in safe places), and bring a friend to get even better results. More connectedness is always good! Bring your partner and children sometimes. It's great for them too! Walking is a wonderful family activity, a great time to talk and have fun while exercising! But remember, you need personal time too, so make sure you save some walking time just for you!

Balance

So, now that we are exercising and healthy, practicing preventative medicine instead of interventive medicine, we need to ensure that we are balanced! There are countless demands on us all so we have to choose carefully. Too many of us, too frequently, cannot say no. There are major categories we need to pay attention to: Health [physical, mental and spiritual], Family, Friends, Work, and Fun! Women, in particular, are very vulnerable to being peace makers and accommodators. We often do things that really are not on our priority list. It can be very difficult saying no to a colleague, a friend or family member, but many times it is the correct thing to do. We at times, for some reason, feel that we have to agree to all that is asked of us or else we are letting others down. They may even be things we want to do. But by overextending ourselves, doing things we don't particularly enjoy and that are not very important, we really only shortchange ourselves. If the demand or request is not in our five categories of priorities, or one category is way too full to busting, then it has to be reconsidered.

Standing up for ourselves can be difficult if we are rather non-confrontational by nature, but it is necessary, especially if we are to achieve personal balance. Maybe we need more recreation in our life, or exercise, friends, or alone time. Being an attentive, involved parent is very absorbing, fun and rewarding as well, but can be very time consuming. So taking a bit of time for yourself is important to keep yourself balanced and fulfilled, healthy and happy. This is essential to being a healthy parent and fostering a healthy family. Remember, we lead by example!

I see many parents living parallel lives to their children. It's usually not intentional and evolves innocently. Parents often themselves are so busy and over scheduled that they do the same to their children. Often the most time they "spend" together is driving to activities. Families in which both parents work, or single parent families, often involve parents working until early evening. "Stay-at-home parents" can also often get too wrapped up in the day to day grind and get very busy very quickly. As a result, parents see their children very briefly before a scheduled activity - hockey, music, swimming, whatever the event - and then before you know it, it's bedtime! We must make good decisions about how we use and share our time together, because before you know it, you'll have all the time in the world and be longing for some time with your children. None of us are here forever, not even for long. If you have lost someone in your life you know this all to well. Be aware of how short 24 hours are, how quickly 15 years pass, and how important it is to make very good use of your time.

Stay Focused

Be in the moment with your children as much as you can. It is not easy to block out distractions, worries or anxieties. The phone rings, you remember something you had to do, yesterday, and get derailed from the present. Make the time you have planned with your children 'protected time', as we call it in academic medicine, and turn off your pager, cell phone, home phone, whatever you can. The world will continue its spinning without you, and when you rejoin, it will all be there for you. The difference is that you will just have spent some great quality time with your children, which will make you all feel better. When we are focused on one event, one person or group at a time, it pays off. We are better able to tackle the next event with more focus and effectiveness, as we feel more satisfied and less distracted now from what we just did. Because we were in the moment, we did what we wanted and did it well. No regrets, second guessing, or wondering if we could have done it better. We did it, focused on it and then moved on with satisfaction. Being more focused on one event naturally leads to more satisfaction for the next event. Whether that event is a work assignment, a quiet conversation with our daughter, or a monopoly game with the whole gang, being focused on it increases its quality remarkably! Staying present actually takes care of the future!

Making Choices

Our environment is also very much more under our control than we realize. We all know instinctively how the "wrong crowd', the

Chapter One • Be Healthy, Have Fun!

wrong music and so on, can so negatively influence our children, but what about us? We also need to be very aware of the influences in our lives. Our work environment, home surroundings and atmosphere, the people we socialize with, our close friends, the music we listen to, and the books we read all have impact. Remember back to a movie you found to be inspiring - how powerful a simple movie can be! If a movie can influence us, just think how much real people can touch us! Our brains absorb our surroundings and accommodate to adjust to the environment, to survive it, to thrive in it. Just think back on some different social situations where you may have acted one way, and another situation where you behaved rather differently. We all adjust to our environment, acting differently with one set of friends than another perhaps. We are also more formal at work, more diplomatic in front of company and so on! Think back to high school; we all acted a bit tougher around the tough group, to survive it, to avoid being teased. We intuitively know how to survive, so we act accordingly. Our brains naturally adapt. We need to pay attention to what is good for us: people, places and activities that complement us, that bring out our best, should be sought out to help us be our best.

So now that we, as parents, all grown up, have more control over who we socialize with, where we go, what we read or listen to, we should make choices, whenever able, to be around people and things that bring out the best in us. Being around positive, enthusiastic people helps us feel the same way, just as being around negativity breeds the same. We have choices, so let's make good ones for ourselves. There are some situations we have to make the most of, but more often we have more control than we care to admit. Making good choices takes sacrifice sometimes at another level. Be determined to take control of your environment!

Our Personal Inventory

Ah, now our emotional selves. Talk about low on the totem pole! We are often so busy that we don't really even take note as to how we are feeling. We seldom stop and check in with ourselves about our emotions. Are we feeling mostly happy, sad, fulfilled, frustrated, or whatever? We usually only start noticing our mood if we are particularly irritable, not sleeping, overeating, or engaging in some other undesirable behaviour. Often other people will notice something in us - our partner may comment that we seem distant or snappy, short with the children, or not interested in intimacy. Our children may complain we are yelling at them. Emotional issues can have many causes. By the way, yelling is a great sign that things are not right. Pay attention to this: yelling makes us and our children feel bad, really bad.

If you are not feeling your best, go see someone about it. As physicians we first need to rule out organic causes, something physical, like a thyroid problem. Unfortunately, hypothyroid issues are common and can cause fatigue, as well as other physical symptoms like cold intolerance, weight gain, constipation and dry skin, to name a few. It can also cause depression. So once again we need to be paying attention to how we are feeling. If something is not right, look into it. You should be feeling energetic and happy for the most part. If you are not, there could be a minor adjustment needed like more sleep or a better diet, or it could be something as serious as a depressive illness.

Depression is a medical condition that affects 10% of men and 20% of women at some point in their lives. Those with any medical conditions are more vulnerable to depression, but it can affect any of us. Again, depression needs to be investigated thoroughly to rule out a physical cause, and psychological stressors need to be explored. There may be something we can do to quickly resolve the issue, or at least explore to help the healing process. Depression can creep up on us or hit us quickly. Listen to close friends and family if they note something is off with you, and look into it. You deserve to be healthy and feel vibrant and alive!

Don't allow your Ego, often full of pride or shame and other destructive feelings, to prevent you from seeking medical attention. If your leg was swollen or your eyesight failing you would likely seek help. Why not also strive for a healthy brain and emotional state? Remember, we need to be healthy and emotionally well to be the best parent and person we can be. Depressive symptoms can wreak havoc on relationships, work, and of course, overall health. Listen to yourself, check in with yourself and pay attention. It pays off! You and your family are the winners when Mom and Dad are feeling at their best. We are better able to pay attention to issues, to have the energy to advocate for our children and be active in their lives, as well as our own, when we as parents are well.

Social Connectedness

Now, relationships! Do you actually have any left? It can get somewhat isolating raising a family. We can get so focused on the day-to-day grind that we often neglect our once close friends and family members. At different phases in our lives we can be more proactive in the initiating of social contacts than at other times. Our friendships are important to help us feel connected, supported, and valued. By maintaining close connections, we have someone to have fun with, to laugh with, which can really be the best medicine many times. If we don't maintain our relationships, it's harder for us to call up someone we haven't spoken with for some time and look for support. The result: we don't, and then we are isolated. Laughter and having fun are as important as having a confidante.

Our various friends usually fulfill different roles for us, and that's fine. So keep yourself connected with various friends. Contacts don't have to be lengthy; most of us just don't have that kind of time. But quick calls, short visits or a quick tea break can go a long way in maintaining contacts. Sometimes we will alternate with friends regarding who is better at keeping up the contact, depending on what is happening in our lives, young children, elderly or sick parents, or a smooth period. Don't be afraid to be the initiator; our turns come around eventually in both roles! We need our friends, in good times and in bad. Having friends helps us keep our own identity, helps us be our own person, which can be easily lost in the busy life of family.

A social connectedness with our friends not only helps our soul, but collaborating with friends about parenting issues can also be helpful! Sharing ideas and learning from each other can be very inspirational. Sometimes we get stuck thinking about a situation in one dimension. We convince ourselves that there is really only one way around a particular issue. Just try to recall a situation in the past about which you felt very strongly; you were adamant about what had to be done or happen in order for you to be happy. Then some time later you looked back and said, "Wow, I can't believe I did that," or "I was so hung up about that (or him or her even!)". Our perspective can change when we least expect it.

So, the next time you feel stuck about an important issue, try imagining an alternate scenario or outcome. We can become rigid about what things, situations, or people should be, but where do we get those preconceived notions? Perhaps a rigid society, a lack of experience, fear even may be a factor. People can be very fearful of change, but change can bring great opportunity. Discussing things of importance that are taxing us with a friend may help challenge our preset mindset about it. Perhaps laughing

Chapter One • Be Healthy, Have Fun!

about it can help us see the whole situation in a different light. Becoming more open minded and flexible about life in general can lift many burdens. Friends can help us broaden our scope of thinking and help us feel supported and light-hearted all at once! It's free psychotherapy that we all need!

Self-Advocate

One of the danger zones I see people entering is living their lives based on the expectations of others. Passive, non-confrontational people can really fall deep into this rut, but even those who are usually good at self-advocating can carry a very heavy white flag! Always being the peace maker or adjusting to others' needs or wants can be very damaging to our own self-development and happiness. Allowing bad behaviour to be directed at us on a regular basis is pretty well inviting it. Someone once told me there are no bad deals, just bad negotiators! This was about business, but the same can be applied to relationships. This is not to say that you should always be looking for the last word, or that you have to confront every misbehaviour. It is important, however, to decide what you feel is acceptable behaviour and how you want to be treated by others. Sometimes we need to let things go, things we cannot change. Sometimes we need to increase our level of empathy for another person and try to see things from their perspective. This may help you see the situation differently. If, however, there is a pattern of negative behaviour consistently directed your way, it needs to be addressed. At least if you want it to change!

We are not helping ourselves at all by allowing others to treat us poorly, or to not value our needs or opinions, or to be disrespectful to us! All relationships are much healthier for us if we confront (as long as it is safe to do so - putting yourself at risk of harm is never a good idea) and deal with inequities as they arise so it does not appear that we are condoning the unwanted behaviour. After a while, allowing undesirable behaviour can eventually become enabling. This applies to all of our relationships - with our partners, children, siblings, friends or colleagues. If we always allow our spouse to call the agenda without consultation, that will become the norm, no matter how much it may bother us. Spouses can't read minds! If we always allow our children to leave the kitchen in a mess, we will do a lot of dishes. Let people know that you expect to be respected and consulted, and if you stick with it, it will happen.

We can very easily get into the mindset that we have to "put up with it", but by allowing others to 'bully' us, we are not being true to ourselves. We must respect ourselves and expect that of others. We can do this without confrontation and with authority! Others will soon learn our new boundaries, and those who value us will adjust and also benefit from a more meaningful relationship! We will feel more empowered and less stressed when we are standing up for ourselves, as well as building healthy, meaningful relationships. You can be kind and loving, yet still be firm about expecting the same from others. It can be very frustrating reflecting back on a situation in which you were treated unfairly, but it is much more bothersome when we didn't stand up for ourselves. We find ourselves reflecting more on the things we "should have said" back, instead of the initial incident. Self-advocating and standing up for ourselves in a respectful way is very satisfying! It allows us to "let go" of the situation much better.

By becoming skilled in self-advocacy, we role model this to our children. By taking charge of how we allow others to treat us, we show our children the true meaning of self-confidence. We lead by example. By illustrating to our children that we will accept only healthy relationships, respectful boundaries, and appropriate behaviour from others, we teach them these same qualities! As parents we aspire for our children to have healthy, happy relationships, so what better way to ensure this than to emulate this! Imagine what the opposite does! Allowing ourselves to endure bad behaviour from others really sends a powerful message as well - a really bad, powerful message!

Some Suggestions

Some suggested scripts could read like this:

To partner: "I know you are trying hard to make this upcoming vacation really special, and I appreciate all the work you are doing on it! I would love, though, to help out and be part of the planning and decision making. Can we sit down tonight and review the plans so far and discuss what's next to arrange?"

It helps to acknowledge your partner's efforts and good intentions, and then to express what you need or think or want. It's good if you can avoid the BUT word that always seems to discount the positives just said: "Thanks a lot, but no thanks!" That little "but" just kills it!

To partner: "Thanks so much for all you do with the children and around the house! I have noticed that lately your tone of voice with me sounds irritable and sometimes disrespectful! This is not like you, and I miss our nice conversations! Is there anything bothering you? Do we need to discuss something? I would love to get back to how we usually are together!"

To child: "It must be a little stressful starting high school this year! I have noticed that you are a little short-tempered with me lately. I really want to help you with this transition, and it is really important to me that we continue to communicate with respect towards each other. Is there an issue we can discuss today? Let's make a plan for how our communication can improve."

This approach again highlights your awareness and appreciation, as well as what you want from your child. A plan is made to follow-up with the issue. Stating your concerns, pointing out the positive, and having a follow-up plan all help with a better outcome. Think about the message you want to get across, make it clear, point out what works, plan ahead of time how you want it to sound. Even write it down and practice it. It doesn't have to be perfect, but planning can be very effective!

Do your best to be well, although some days it will be easier than others. Rather than feeling guilty because you didn't get as much exercise as you wanted, be grateful that you are now giving yourself some attention. Once you start taking care of yourself it becomes rewarding and motivating. You will soon start to experience benefits like more energy, patience, and creativity. But be patient; remember that it took years to get to this point so it takes at least months to see changes sometimes, depending on your starting point. It took almost a year of yoga for me to start seeing outward benefits, but change inside and in our brains starts immediately. Your attitude about yourself is what is most important; the rest is sure to follow. The benefits ARE in the process.

It's important to note that once you decide to make some of these changes, you may not immediately receive support or understanding from those around you. Don't expect too many accolades of congratulations from colleagues when, after 10 years of working through lunch, you've now decided to eat a nutritious lunch away from your desk and get a quick walk in! Your partner

Chapter One • Be Healthy, Have Fun!

may feel insecure that you've decided to join a gym or dance class, or have stopped putting ironing before a walk after supper. Some people become insecure and even jealous when they see others making good decisions. This may be because they also want to, but don't feel able. Or maybe they see your new set of priorities as selfish or become intimidated by your change. Those who love you will applaud you eventually, and if significant people in your life (like partners or friends and colleagues) don't eventually 'get it", that is their issue to sort out. You can still be responsible to your job and family, as well as be good to yourself. These issues are not mutually exclusive. It's about balance. Sometimes other things have to come first; that's life, juggling the balls. But we can still play ball, for some time each day, no matter how briefly.

Here's a suggestion for how to advocate for yourself about taking your lunch hour at home when no one else in the office does: "I've decided that I really would like to spend my lunch hour at home with my young children. This will really help me feel more productive in the afternoon. I'll ensure I don't go over time, but if that happens occasionally due to unforeseeable issues right now, I will add time to my morning, and I will readdress the whole issue with you. I would really appreciate your support on this!" When you do something 'different' from the rest, people can become defensive, a little jealous, and maybe resentful. So be upfront, explain your reasoning and ask for support. You may not have a full cheerleading team, but if you stay within your rights and responsibilities, you have nothing to feel guilty about. The time well spent will be way more rewarding than false camaraderie at the office lunch table!

Don't feel that you are responsible for convincing all others of the importance of your good self care. That can take up a ton of energy and may make you uncertain of your actions. Act responsibly towards your family, job, and friends, and there's no need to rationalize taking a walk before the dishes, a yoga class once a week, or a 20-minute reading break - just don't expect applause! Your children will likely be the most supportive. Again they have a lot to teach us. They know the value of play, friends, and fun. They know how committed you are to them; they want you to be happy. Lots of children in my practice feel and say that their parents need to pay more attention to themselves and have more fun. When you are connected to your children, they are insightful to your needs and supportive of your efforts to try to meet some of them. My children are usually much more relaxed about me going out for a walk without them or seeing a friend than I am. "You need friends too Mommy," is what they have said. Children are so unselfish, so giving and accommodating. When we see that, we need to respect and nurture it. Don't take advantage of it, but learn from it. We gain so much in return!

Get Informed!

Reading is an amazing way to broaden and challenge our thinking. Self-help books (like this one) are plentiful, and if you find one that you connect with, it can be inspiring. Again, they don't often tell us what we don't instinctively know, but they can be very motivating. They can be informative on topics we haven't read much on, and can help us see things differently. It is really hard to find time for reading as a parent, but if you make it one of your priorities, you will get some done. I was very anti-self-help books for a very long time. I'm a psychiatrist; I thought, what could I read that I haven't already about human behaviour! Plus, I was tired a lot and usually fell into bed at the end of the day.

Then a good friend of mine gave me a book for Christmas, Again, it wasn't saying a lot I didn't know, but it reminded me of how important it is to rebalance and to take good care of one's self. I've read a couple more since then, and I think the greatest benefit is that these books help me think more broadly, to try to see the breadth of options and to seek more options to situations. Books help us open our minds.

There are many ways to get informed these days, the internet being a big one. As parents we need to be informed about technology in order to educate and protect our children, as well as learn to use technology to help inform ourselves when needed!

Having a "reading" time for the whole family can also be helpful. It teaches children of all ages that reading is fun and informative. Even if your 10 year-old doesn't have homework, having a designated reading time that everyone in the family participates in teaches many things; reading is fun, important and sets the stage for good study habits. We can develop good habits as easily as bad habits, so why not work on some good ones!

As part of being your best self, healthy and energetic, also take your parenting pulse. Look at your parenting style, what's working and what's not. Just like our physical or health status, our parenting status needs ongoing assessment and adjusting. I'll discuss in a later chapter how the various stages of growth which our children go through will require adjustments to our parenting style. Our parenting styles will occasionally need tweaking and flexibility.

Family Time

Another often overlooked facet of our personal health and satisfaction is vacation time - what a great concept! Despite what some people might think, a vacation is not a frivolous luxury. It's really an important "together time" for families to have that is not competing with other responsibilities. Work, the telephone, and day-to-day routines in general often take over completely at home. Vacation is time just for you as a family to be together, to be focused on each other, in a relaxed state of mind. It is infinitely easier to be calm, patient, fun, spontaneous, focused, and engaged during a holiday. It's important not only for family to get away together, but for parents to get away for short periods as well. Don't lose sight of how important it is to have happy parents, and happy together if at all possible! All relationships need nurturing to thrive; don't forget the one that started all this! Intimacy strengthens the bond, it helps ground relationships. Pay attention to your relationship with your partner, keep it fun and respectful, and did I say fun? Men and women have different needs, and we need to be mindful of this. By being attentive to your partner's needs, you will find your needs being met quite nicely! A weekend away, just the two of you, can help you get through a lot of homework strife and bottle drives!

Most importantly, remember that, as parents, we are the most significant role models for our children. For everything!

Points to Remember

Exercise daily, eat well, and get enough sleep. The basics of self care often get overlooked and undervalued! Sleep deprivation is a very common cause of crankiness, in children and adults!

Be active in your health care. No one knows you better than you, and no one has the same interest. Self-monitor and investigate when necessary.

Exercise: find something you are passionate about! Exercise is so so good for us, all of us. Regular exercise helps both our minds and bodies. Lots of research supports this.

Balance the demands facing you, choose how you spend your time carefully. Take a few minutes to plan your day, week, and month. It is time well spent.

Control what you can in your environment. Surround yourself with positivity and nurturing. Be around those who complement you, who bring out your best.

Check in with your emotional self. Don't neglect what is so important. Being happy is vital to a happy family.

Collaborate with friends and family. We gain so much from each other.

Don't feel guilty about little issues or for being healthy and balanced. It's a big waste of time.

Read. Especially the next few chapters! Reading helps open our minds, and helps us actually sit and relax!

| Inspired Parenting

"You are joined together with peace through the spirit, so make every effort to continue together in this way."
Ephesians 4.3

Chapter Two

Lessons from my Mentors

I have an amazing yoga teacher, by the name of Barbara. What a coincidence that she is the only other Barbara I have ever really known! Were we meant to meet? I think so. She has given me so much. I could hardly get all the lessons, pearls of wisdom, guidance, and inspiration down on paper, but I feel it is my duty to try! I thank you, Barbara, for being so much to me: the walks, the talks and encouragement, the yoga, and for allowing me to share with others some of you! There are many parallels between yoga and parenting, and life in general. I will try to get some of these similarities across now! I also thank Pamela, my massage therapist at the time, who taught me much, and delivered me to Barbara!

Barbara D.

I started yoga with Barbara nine years ago; I had known Barbara through our research paper, being introduced to her from another amazing woman in my life, Pamela, my massage therapist. Pamela had been encouraging me to join yoga with Barbara for several years. Even though I had one excuse after another for not joining, Pamela did not lose patience with me. She taught me yoga to do at home, she planted the seeds of learning to retrain my body.

She taught me about self-advocacy, self-care, and striving to be strong. She taught me about yoga, and I didn't even know it! So one evening when my son Timothy was nine months old, I was on the phone with Pamela, and once again she was encouraging me to get to yoga. "Just do it!" said Pamela. So I called Barbara, who said, "Come tonight, it's an intermediate class but you'll be OK!" So I went. I didn't miss a class for three years!

I started gaining back confidence in my physical strength; I was gaining energy, and most importantly, overall confidence. By taking on the challenges of the physical pose, or asana, I began building confidence in other areas of my life. Learning that you can do something that seems really difficult - like a yoga pose - with hard work, determination, and focus, spills over into other areas. It helps you take on new challenges with confidence and determination. Barbara also teaches us (her students) to let go: after you have worked on the pose, no matter how it felt, let go of the negative, don't let it bother you, leave it, and move on to the next pose with a fresh start. Barbara teaches students to observe their body, and observe their body in the pose. Don't react to the pain, allow it to be there. Just like I tell my patients, 'you can observe another person's (bad) behaviour, it doesn't mean you have to absorb it'. She teaches us the value of focus, being in the pose, listening to your body, sensing your body, being very aware of yourself in the pose. Don't think about the groceries you have to get, the work left undone, or the situation you just left. Those thoughts do not belong here in the yoga room. It is you and your mat, you and your focus, you and your determination. Very empowering messages, with results! All that from some simple yoga poses? You betcha!

My Yogi, Barbara, started yoga when yoga wasn't sexy. She began over 30 years ago, at a time in our society, especially in

Chapter Two • Lessons from My Mentors

Newfoundland, when women held very traditional roles in families and society. Yoga wasn't popular in Newfoundland at that time. In fact there were only two Yoga teachers, and Barbara didn't even know that! When a book about yoga fell off a shelf at her feet at the library, she was hooked. With four small children and a very busy life, Barbara stepped out of her world of strict expectations and broke the mold - my kind of woman!! She knew what she needed in her life and broke all the rules to pursue the noble cause of good, healthy self-care. She didn't hurt anyone else, she didn't neglect her family duties, but she took a very new course, a very new approach, and did what was right for her. Barbara had to be creative, brave, and very determined. She had to seek out opportunities to learn and practice yoga. She found like- minded people and made the time for herself. All this when she was really just expected to look after the children, attend to her marriage, and be what everyone expected. Well she did all that and more, because once she started taking good care of herself, her strength grew, her confidence grew, and her family reaped many rewards from this, as have all her students.

Anyone who knows Barbara is blessed by her amazing perseverance, her knowledge, and wisdom. She teaches her students with a sincerity and energy beyond description. She leads by example, she does poses I am still not close to mastering, even after nine years of yoga. She is dedicated to her practice, and she shows us that yoga, like life, evolves. Some days are better than others; some days we are all more balanced, more focused, or just stronger. Somedays we need to be more forgiving of ourselves and others. We never stop trying, we keep pushing through, even on the tough days, even through the tough poses. We don't give up. Well, she just won't let us!

Learning from Barbara

So, if Barbara can do it, can break away from the grind of others' expectations, break away from society's pull toward tradition, and overcome personal challenges to do yoga, when yoga wasn't even really happening in her home town, can't we go for a walk?! In speaking with Barbara about families, she agrees that parents get so tied up with family issues that she sees people losing themselves. She sees how vital it is to take care of oneself, to be healthy and strong. She knows herself the demands of parenting - she has four children, and her children have children. She knows exactly what it's like to be pulled in 14 directions. That is precisely why self-care is so important. To be available to others, you need to be available to yourself first. Parents are more than parents; they are people too! That person needs to be healthy to be a good parent. She sees how many of us get very caught up in daily stressors, the many demands and how we get very distracted from the now.

When I asked Barbara to comment on how she feels we can be more calm and grounded, she replied:

"Firstly I think people are not taking time for themselves. A half an hour in the morning, in the night, just to read something spiritual, to meditate, or to do some yoga, whatever, just a half an hour a day to yourself can make a big difference! Before you get into the day, take time for yourself. I think this is calming, it allows your body to wake up, and meditation definitely helps you deal with the business of the mind all day. We have 24 hours in a day; we sleep for about 8 hours, and we work for about 8 hours, so what are we doing for the rest of the time? Can we not find a half an hour to self-reflect, to touch base with ourselves? Start with just 5 minutes of quiet time; it can change your whole perspective on things!"

Chapter Two • Lessons from My Mentors

I fully agree! Taking some quiet time allows us to be calmer. Even the intention to meditate, especially for us beginners in that area, helps tremendously in clearing our mind for the whole day! The results are really quite startling!

Part of yoga is accepting our bodies, respecting our limitations, and working with what we've got. These principles also apply to how we should approach our children. Acceptance, respect, and hard work are needed to help reach a child's potential. Our children are gifts to us.

Barbara said, *"We think we can mold our children as we want them, but that doesn't always work! Our children come into this world with their own mission, and they need to find out what they need to do to grow into better people. to move forward."*

Children are very incredible. They are very individually wired; they need our guidance and support, our patience and wisdom. Our children need our respect for who they are.

A big challenge for me is learning how to practice yoga at home as diligently as I work in class with Barbara, how to take that focus and determination and ignite it all by myself. To push myself where I need to go, all on my own. To practice with integrity, honesty, and determination. When no one is watching or pushing me. Just me and my mat, just me and my focus, just me and my determination. Don't use excuses, don't look for compromise, and don't cheat yourself out of the benefits. That's what she teaches us. By doing it (the pose) correctly, with honest effort, we reap the rewards. By cheating, we lose. By allowing ourselves to get away with doing the least possible, we lose. It is simple. There is so much to gain by doing it correctly, with some effort and determination. By not paying attention, by not putting our effort in the right direction, we don't get the full benefit. We lose out. Sounds like parenting to me!

Get Passionate!

Barbara and her yoga instruction have been invaluable to me. Finding Barbara has been a gift. A gift I accepted and went with. I recognized the value of yoga for me and the teachings of my mentor. Allow yourself to be open to change, to get connected to others, and try new things. There is something for everyone: dance, martial arts, hiking, the list is endless. We just have to find it, and to find it, you have to be looking! So if you have a passion, have fun with it. If you are looking for a passion, don't give up until you find it. It is out there, as are the rewards.

Mentors

Mentors are people we can find anywhere. I have had many. All of my friends have inspired me in some way; they all have something to teach me. The people I work with help guide me, teach me. Everyone has something to give, something to teach; we only need to be open to their gifts. I am thankful for everyone in my life, for their gifts to me! My sisters and brother have been wonderful mentors, and of course my parents have been my biggest inspiration, along with my own children. My husband teaches me something every day. Our mentors are many.

If you need direction in a certain area, seek out someone you admire, connect with, trust, and feel can help you in this particular skill. Talk to them, explain what you want help with, and see if they can help. Mentoring comes in many styles, some formal, some subtle, and most in between. I have been very blessed with many mentors. We all have them actually. Some we must seek more actively, but most are in our midst already; we just have to recognize them! How does that saying go: "Ask and you shall receive!"

So I asked my very wise father of five, what was his advice to parents, and he replied, " It is important to recognize each child in the family as unique, and treat them all with the same respect and compassion." A very loving and insightful father, who continues to teach me about love and parenting.

Points to remember

There are amazing people everywhere. Recognizing them is key!

Once you recognize someone you find inspiring, allow yourself to learn from them, share with them.

Yoga is amazing! Find your amazing thing, it's out there!

Thank you to my Mentors!

> *"Blessed are the ones God sends to show His love for us."*
> *Fr. JJM*

Chapter Three

Kindness and Other Things Undervalued

Kindness at Home

Kindness is sometimes a trait we associate with visions like Little Bo Peep and, unfortunately, is sometimes seen as a kind of weakness. We don't often stress the importance of this characteristic to our children, I think because we don't want them to be taken advantage of. As adults, a lot of us think we may be past the need to utilize this human behaviour and have undervalued it. Perhaps our kindnesses have not been justly recognized or rewarded. Maybe our kindness was exploited. Kindness is vulnerable, not always reciprocated, and can leave us open to feeling hurt if not recognized. But kindness can also be heroic, life-changing, and self-rewarding. It can be quiet and subtle, life-saving, and self-preserving. It can define us and protect us. It is a humanistic trait that is diminishing in our competitive world, saved for special events and recipients, and unfortunately seen as monumental by some. But really, it is simple, uncomplicated, and necessary for truly warm, sincere relationships.

Chapter Three • Kindness and Other Things Undervalued!

Kindness should be the everyday stuff, and it should start at home, which is often the place where people find it most difficult to be nice, kind, and polite. We tend to take our troubles out at home, where we feel safe. But it is here we also need to cultivate peace, kindness, and love. It is truly important that parents role model kindness in order for children to live it and practice it. Small acts of kindness all help: picking up one another's plate from the table, closing their bedroom door to let them sleep after a late night, offering to cook supper for a change. Day-to-day kindnesses teach us respect and consideration. When we extend kindness, especially as parents, it usually bounces back to us. We teach our children that kindness reflects caring and compassion, not weakness. There isn't a score board in the kitchen – it's give and take.

There is a big difference between being kind and being taken advantage of. Respect for each other is key and, when this is present, kindness is easy and not exploited. Kindness to each other is essential for closeness and tenderness. When it is lacking, the bonds are not as strong as they could be. Kindness is a combination of many things like respect, consideration, thoughtfulness, sacrifice, and forgiveness. These qualities reflect the gentle side of us, the nurturing and loving side. Without these qualities, we are missing out enormously in our relationships.

As parents, we need to self-reflect and check to see how we are doing in this category. How do we rank with respect to these traits with our spouse, children, and extended family? How do we approach neighbours, visitors, friends, and how about the family dog? Remember, our children are watching us very carefully. Treat as you want to be treated. It sounds so simple, and it is. At home we tend to speak very freely, sometimes too freely. The flip side of kindness could be criticism or judgment. Sometimes casual, impulsive comments made at home about others may reflect this rather unkind perspective and boy, once said, forever remembered by little ears. Oh yes, and repeated! Usually we don't even really mean what we say impulsively. We may be tired, frustrated, or whatever, but not thoughtful. So be careful. Home is where the heart is, and the ears!

Worldly Kindness

Now, how do we take kindness outside to play? That partly depends on who we are playing with, where and what the starting point is. Our children are all different in their temperaments, their vulnerability and abilities to navigate through the challenges of life. Some children are very soft-hearted and almost too kind at times. These children are easily hurt, open to being taken advantage of, and need coaching on how to direct their kindness in the appropriate direction. We don't want to dampen the kindness of these children, but they require some assistance in how to recognize their disposition and need to be educated on how to be realistic on the spectrum of how others receive kindness. In order to attempt to try to prevent them from being hurt, we need to help them temper kindness with emotional savvy to know how to prevent disaster!

Children, who are so open, loving and kind, are so pure, unsuspecting and a joy to be around. They are kind to younger children. They are playful and often enthusiastic. It seems so unkind to not help them channel this beautiful spirit. It is not the intention to change them, but only to gently assist them in gaining insight into human nature and interactions. For example, if your daughter experiences unsolicited harshness from a "friend" to whom she has been very kind, it is important to explain that every person is responsible for her own behaviour. When someone is unkind, it is because of her personality and circumstances. Explain to your daughter that it is not something she did, as she cannot 'cause' anyone to act a

Chapter Three • Kindness and Other Things Undervalued!

certain way; it was her 'friend's' decision to be unkind. Help her see who owns the behaviour.

Learning to navigate through human behaviour - the good, the bad and the ugly - becomes more of an issue when your bundle of kindness starts school. Slowly but surely the often aggressive atmosphere of school becomes a little, or a lot, unkind. The group mentality can be very different from the sweet individual. We see it as adults - power in numbers, the office persona - so why should innocent children be immune from this societal phenomenon? Some of our children are less inclined to be kind. Some are very competitive, a little aggressive, or insecure and defensive. These children need a little, or a lot, of help being outwardly or openly kind. These children are a little less confident or comfortable with overt kindness. Sometimes children don't understand how great little acts of kindness make others feel and how empowering they really are, and need more education and encouragement. Children are innately good. Sometimes personality traits they have inherited, or a medical condition they may have, make the appreciation or displaying of kindness more challenging, but it is always possible.

So the education of our children about kindness is complicated. We need to help them understand that kindness is important, is based on respect of others, and will not always be returned, at least not right away. We need to teach them that kindness is not a sign of weakness and that the true reward for kindness is our own self-satisfaction in knowing we did the right thing. Picking up for the underdog, not leaving others out, staying away from exclusion groups - the opportunities for instructive parenting are endless. We need to be paying attention to the peer dynamics. Watch your child interact with his or her friends. Afterwards have a brief discussion, look for opportunities to praise them, and make suggestions. Ask them how it went, use the word kindness, and see if they recognize it in themselves and others. Ask how things could have been better. If we are paying attention, there is a ton of material to work with! Every day is an opportunity for teaching and appreciating our children.

Understanding Others

Teaching children about empathy is a good way to help them develop and understand the concept of kindness. Empathy is the ability to understand how another person is feeling and how they are experiencing a situation. In other words, it is the ability to put yourself in someone else's shoes. This requires some teaching by parents, as it requires some abstract thinking, which isn't easy for young children. Some children find it easier than others, and some need more explanation. It's good practice for parents to bring up the concept of empathy on a regular basis. By helping your child learn to understand and appreciate another person's perspective, you are helping him learn how to navigate through relationships and how to relate better to others.

This ability to relate to and understand others is called emotional intelligence. The better we understand where other people are coming from, the more open-minded, flexible and understanding we are, and usually the better we are able to be kind. We tolerate situations and people better when we understand them. We don't have to share their point of view, but we can appreciate it better when we understand it. When we are not threatened by someone, not defensive about something or insecure, we are more open to understanding him or her.

For example, when we are trying to help our 13 year-old daughter understand why her previous best friend has been unkind to her by excluding her from a social event, we help her understand why

Chapter Three • Kindness and Other Things Undervalued!

her friend may see this move as important, and what it is about her friend that may have contributed to this behaviour. We help point out some of the reasons for this behaviour; we are not excusing the behaviour but helping explain it. This allows our child to see the situation for what it is and helps alleviate the negative emotions that may interfere with her own natural kindness, yet also helps prevent her or her kindness from being exploited. By understanding why someone may act in anger, jealousy, fear, aggression, or in some other negative way, the child can allow the other person to own the behaviour and feel less impacted by it. Helping a child understand why someone may act in a certain manner helps them understand the situation and person better, and to react in a more understanding nature, without personalizing the other person's behaviour, even if this behaviour is directed towards her. This is not to excuse bad behaviour, but to help better understand it.

When a child feels less victimized and angry about a situation and understands, "it's them, not me", when applicable, it saves them some cynicism and hardening. It helps them develop insight into the spectrum of human behaviour without taking on the responsibility of others' behaviour. Another good way of helping our child understand human emotions and behaviour is to ask our child how his classmate or friend may have felt when a particular behaviour or event took place. This is easy everyday chitchat on the way home from school or at supper when the day's events are reviewed. So when your son reports that his grade two classmate cried in class when the teacher asked him to explain why his math sheet wasn't completed, and you ask him how his peer must have been feeling and some of the possibilities on why, you are helping your child see the situation from the inside out. You are helping him see the numerous possibilities of why that situation may have happened and how his classmate may have felt. He will likely relate to some of the possible explanations and likely feel more compassion and understanding for his friend. This conversation may only take minutes for you, but go miles in helping your child develop compassion and understanding for others!

Be Self Aware, Then Instructive

Kindness is not without sacrifice, which, in our day of immediate gratification, can be difficult to teach. But it does need to be taught, reinforced, and role modeled. Parents need to supplement their children's' innate kindness streak. Our children need some help in recognizing kindness and its importance, self-monitoring their kindness, and navigating through others' treatment of their kindness. We need to help them be good self-advocates, as well as kind people. They need to learn not to be taken advantage of, without learning cynicism. To trust without being gullible. To appreciate without judgment, yet understand realities. We can make this stuff complicated or simple, depending on how well we understand and explain it ourselves. Often we just need to try to see things as simply as possible, while trying to let go of the biases we hold.

The ability to teach and role model kindness is so utterly dependent on how we as parents really get it. This is certainly a great opportunity for us to self-reflect. What is our bias, our temperament? Are we a little cynical, mistrusting, defensive, insecure, or judgmental? Are we too trusting, gullible, open, and vulnerable to waving the white flag a bit too much? No one else is listening here, so try to be honest with yourself. If you really don't know where you rank on the kindness scale, use a lifeline and ask a friend. Be open to what you hear; it may be very helpful.

Instead of asking another, you may just want to look inside closely, because when we are a little 'this' or 'that', our children

Chapter Three • Kindness and Other Things Undervalued!

usually get it in bigger, more exaggerated doses. The trait is yet to be tempered in our children. They need our guidance in refining and understanding their personalities. Remember that kindness is underrated, misunderstood, and often lacking. It could be the salvation of relationships, true happiness, and a peaceful world. Isn't that on most of our wish lists for our children? So pay attention to it, learn how to foster it and how to be it. Your children will benefit directly from your kindness, reciprocate it, and make you feel better too! Their relationships will be more meaningful, and they will experience more self-fulfillment. That's a lot of stuff for one little word, kindness!

Points to remember

Kindness is important and often undervalued.

Kindness can be cultivated, and we as parents can teach our children how to use it wisely.

Kindness adds to the quality of our relationships.

Kindness bounces back nicely. Parental role modeling of kindness is the most powerful teaching tool.

Teach your children to understand self-ownership of behaviour, especially when kindness is not reciprocated.

> *"Let no one ever come to you without leaving better and happier."*
> Mother Theresa of Calcutta

Chapter Four

Respect

R-E-S-P-E-C-T! Wasn't there a song made about this word? Well it is extremely important to all relationships, especially the ones with our children. When someone feels respected, they feel valued and important which feeds their sense of self and the all-important self esteem. This is especially important for children. As a child's relationship with their parents is their most important, most validating relationship, we play a big role here. As parents, we are often looking for ways to help our child's self esteem, and our own relationship with them is the place to start. Inflated praise for routine basics is often misinterpreted as a great way to make a child feel self worth, but that often really only generates false self expectations. However, when we treat our children with respect, it teaches them true self value. It's good for them, and it's good for us. The topic of respect will resurface a few times in this book; it's hard to avoid it when talking about healthy relationships.

You, the Teacher, Again!

Remember, we teach through example, so when we use manners and respect the needs and rights of our children as individuals, this helps illustrate our respect for them. When we treat with respect, we can expect respect back! When you make a request of your child with 'please', it shows that you appreciate their compliance, even when you are asking them to do what you should expect of them. So when you say, "Peter, please make your bed, we have to go soon and you need to get that done, thank you", your child feels more respected and appreciated. It's hard to always remember our manners, but if we try hard, they will be present most of the time. Our children will follow our lead, and, with polite reminders, they will do well with this. Using manners is not just a formality; it actually builds genuine respect for one another. By teaching our children to be mannerly, we give them an edge in life. Children who are mannerly get noticed, they stand out, especially when they are sincere. When a child is truly respectful and using appropriate manners, they are conveying a quality that people notice and like. People in general want to be valued, and when a child addresses someone with manners, they convey this message. "What you are saying to me matters" is what comes across. So when you teach your child to greet people politely, to make eye contact, to sit down and visit with company for a few moments, or say 'pardon' instead of 'what', you are helping them with their interpersonal connections tremendously. They will definitely be more endearing to others, and at home they will be working towards very healthy relationships!

Validation

Another way to treat our children with respect is to understand that they have rights to feel protected, loved, and have the right to choice, within safety parameters. So offer choice when appropriate and allow freedom of self-expression about an issue and discuss it. When we listen to their point of view, we just may see the situation differently. Allowing your child to have a voice validates their thoughts and feelings. It helps them feel worthwhile, that their opinion matters. It makes a difference! This process of validating a child's point of view promotes self worth, develops a deeper self-awareness and feelings of appropriate entitlement, entitlement of being heard. They do matter, they have things to offer, and their opinions are helpful. This in turn helps children have the confidence to seek what they need, to look for answers, and to be an active player in their life. It starts small - listening, respecting one another - and grows big!

This is not to say we need to negotiate everything or we wouldn't get out of the house! When things are non-negotiable, say that and remain firm. Your children will learn to respect your authority when you drop the ambivalence over non-negotiable issues and become more flexible and open-minded about negotiable issues. I tell parents to be up front on this issue. Tell your children if something is non-negotiable and not up for discussion, or if it is negotiable and you will consider their input. As the parent, you don't always have to make a decision right away; you can defer your decision until you've had time to consider the matter or discuss it with your partner later. If your children know that you will be fair and respectful about decision-making, it will make it easier for them to delay the decision. Children can have significant trouble delaying their gratification, so respectful firmness is often in order!

Communicating Respect

Attitude and tone are essential ingredients to respect and respectful communication. We easily recognize poor attitude and disrespect in others, but do we see it as easily in ourselves? Not usually. Often we are defensive when someone tells us we sound upset or sarcastic. We snap back quickly to deny the supposed emotion, usually too quickly. If someone is experiencing our tone, body language, words, or attitude as something unintended, then we should pay attention. We can get into some nasty patterns of communication at home that are very far from respectful. We may not answer people, we may walk away, storm away, use sarcasm, even ridicule and belittle. A roll of the eye, a mutter under your breath - these gestures exude disrespect. Sounds awful doesn't it, but it happens a lot!

I see parents calling their children 'playful" derogatory names, criticizing their honest efforts and expressing dissatisfaction when not necessary. Sounds like bullying, and it is bullying. Most parents don't intend for their 'joking around' to be taken seriously or see it as having an impact on their child, but it definitely does, especially when done frequently. This happens to the best of us, particularly if we are stressed, tired or angry, which is not unusual when in a dispute or "discussion" with a family member. But however unintentional this thoughtless form of communication may be, it can be damaging, very damaging, to the child's self concept. The child may feel they cannot please the parent and so gives up trying. They may feel ineffective, devalued, and this can have definite consequences on their relationships and communication style. Parental modeling of respect will ultimately affect their children's relationships - their relationship with them and others.

Our communication style can have dramatic impact on our quality of relationships, on how our children communicate with the world, and on the emotional health of our children. Speak to your children as you want them to speak to you. Listen to them as you want them to listen to you. Respect them, and they will respect you. There is a monumental difference between fearing and respecting your parent. A nice way of acknowledging your child's effort may sound like this: "Thank you so much Catherine for helping me prepare supper. It meant a lot to me for you to help out and put off going out with your friend. It's also great to spend time with you! If you need a drive over to Cindy's later, let me know!"

Discipline is vital, and when done with respect and consistency, it will be respected. Say to your children what you mean, and mean what you say. Being firm and in control is essential for your children to feel secure in your parenting, your protecting. Children require direction and boundaries; they need our guidance. Done with respect, providing discipline to our children will be rewarding for us and them. Children will not always agree with our decisions, and they will protest at times. That's their job. And it's our job to try to make good, sound decisions, with respect, for our children. We won't always be absolutely correct. If you are unsure of a decision, delay the verdict on the issue. If you are ambivalent about a decision, your children will pick up on that immediately, whether they are 2 or 22 years-old! So maybe you need to wait for backup or a good night's sleep! That's okay, sometimes we need to wait. Make the best decisions you can with the information you have at the time. Mix that with your respect for your children, and you will do well. Modeling calm, thoughtful decision-making will teach your child to do the same.

Be patient with your children and yourself. If you make a mistake, which is inevitable, acknowledge it and say sorry, then move on! An apology could sound like this, after you may have lost it over something less than life-threatening: "Listen kids, I'm sorry I got really mad at you guys for [dropping my cell phone in the toilet]! I said things that I shouldn't have, and you didn't deserve it. I am upset about the phone, but accidents happen, and I know you didn't mean it. So I hope you forgive me! Next time please be more careful and respectful of my belongings! Now let's go pick Mommy out a new cell phone!"

When we resort to out-of-control disciplining, yelling, and stomping, firstly we are role modeling what we DON'T want them to do. Second, it means WE are out of control (more than our child usually) and then usually we feel guilty and overcompensate and give in to something we probably shouldn't! So take a breath if you feel really mad, count, take a walk, take what you need to feel more calm and in control, and then try to communicate clearly and calmly. Pretend someone you want to impress is watching! Do your best, and keep in mind you must communicate with respect and address issues BEFORE they get out of control.

Adult Zone

Being respectful to our children AND partner (our children are watching!!) is vital to a happy household, solid relationships, and confident children. It is also essential for preparing our children for life! Children who have the ability to communicate with respect at home will also do so out in the world. What our children learn at home stays with them forever. Communicating with respect will give them the respect of others. Our children are our future, our ability for us to leave an imprint on the world. So a part of us lives on, and hopefully we have helped impart the skills for them to have a successful, happy, and healthy life. Inter-parental communication, how Mommy and Daddy speak and communicate to each other, will teach our children a lot, good and bad, depending on what they see! Remember that children see their parents interact together more than any other two people, so they are learning a lot from you about how to communicate to others. Children will speak to siblings very similarly to how parents communicate with each other. Children will react to stress very similarly to how parents react. When I am speaking to patients and families about communication issues, I ask who the child speaks and communicates like. It's always like one or both parents! Go figure!

Chapter Four • Respect

I tell my patients over and over again that the only person's behaviour they can control is their own. Same for adults and spouses/partners. If you are struggling with issues of communication and respect in your home, your best approach is to lead by example. It is important for both men and women to remember that the different sexes do have different styles of communicating, due primarily to our hard wiring and, of course, our societal influences on gender. If there are two parents or other parental figures in the home, we need to be somewhat tolerant of each other's individual approach. Respect needs to happen on all fronts and, hopefully, in all relationships, but it may come across a little differently from different parental figures. Men may find women are a little soft, and women may find men a little too direct. I know I find the male wrestling a little unnerving at times, but then love it when I am actually in the ring! Our children benefit from both parents, when possible, to be involved. As long as these relationships are healthy and of course respectful, they need to be supported.

When there is strife between parents, very unfortunately the adults may play 'tug-of- child', knowing that for most parents their softest, most sensitive spot is their children. So an unhappy spouse may try winning parental points with a child by trying to monopolize their time and attention, or try to discredit the other parent. The victim here is always the child. A healthy child needs healthy relationships with both parents, whenever possible, no matter what the parental state of affairs, and if this is damaged, it is the child who truly loses out. So if there is strife, try very hard to keep the children out of it. This is much easier said than done, but even little innuendoes and slights to the other parent are felt as hurt by the child. Be aware and gentle. It is not easy stuff to navigate through, so reassess, ask for guidance, and remember some days are better than others!

Everyday Benefits

Think about what clear, respectful communication can do in your everyday relationships. In general, people want to be listened to and respected, and if you've taught your child how to do that, it is a big accomplishment! It will carry them well through life in every arena. One can be assertive and a leader most effectively through gaining respect. A child who has felt respected at home learns he/she is deserving of respect and should expect it from others, as well as treat others with such. This helps us all, from ages 7- 97, to reject bullying, disrespect, and poor behaviour from others, as well as ourselves! We can stay out of trouble most of the time by treating those with whom we are interacting with kindness and respect, including respecting ourselves!

In my clinical practice, regardless of the presenting issue for the child and family, when there is good respect between family members, it makes working through issues much easier. When there is disrespect, it is much more difficult to make progress, and the whole respect issue needs to be addressed first. Lots of times there are communication issues between teens and parents, but as long as there is underlying respect, the communication eventually improves. When I see disrespect between family members, there is often a lack of motivation to finding a solution. A lack of respect often translates into not believing the other person and not really appreciating what they may be going through. Parents may feel their child is embellishing their troubles and looking for sympathy. Children may feel their parents don't care about them or their problems. They can also have difficulty seeing things from their parent's perspective. If a person doesn't feel respected, they are likely to think that the other person doesn't really care. That is usually not the case, but perception becomes that person's reality.

Chapter Four • Respect

When we don't feel respected by someone, it is hard to respect them back. It is simple math, one and one makes two: one respectful gesture creates another. If things are not going well, take it one respectful act at a time. The first step is to recognize that respect may be lacking and make steps to change the way you speak to that person. Where does it all start? When do we start the pattern of behaviour that leads to things going in the wrong direction? Disrespectful behaviour often starts slowly, unintentionally, but can be very hurtful if we don't recognize its destructive power.

I see a lot of wonderful children and teens in my practice. Some of these people would be described by their teachers or parents as disrespectful, hot-tempered, or oppositional. But usually in my office they are polite, they apologize for swearing if they slip, they are sorry if they are late, and they thank me when leaving. So how does this happen? I know there is the emotional disconnect; I am not their parent or teacher, but I do have expectations. I think that their display of respectful behaviour is a nice example of the equation: treat with respect, receive respect. I always expect that the children and teens I see will be respectful, and I treat them with respect. It is a clean slate in my office, a new beginning. The simple words of please, thank you, it is nice to meet you, and an attitude of concern and validation - easy, respectful gestures. Sincere. When teenagers and children experience this, they give back in kind. So when you want to turn things around with your child, start a new beginning in your mind. Clear the slate, start over. It can certainly be difficult to clean off the emotional slate - it's sticky and hard to clean - but you can. Let go of the negative, the frustration. There is nothing of value to lose there! Over a lifetime, we could benefit from this exercise over and over. We have nothing to benefit from holding onto the negative, especially with our children.

Turning things around can be easy. A simple thank you can be very powerful. Asking permission to enter a teen's room reminds them that you respect their space and privacy and that they are important to you. A simple apology can be very powerful. Sorry can be the hardest thing to say, but it has lots of impact and can change everything. If you wish to clear the air with your child, consider saying something like this: "Jonathon, I've noticed that lately we are not speaking very respectfully to each other. I want you to know that I do respect you and your opinions, but sometimes I have to be the one to make unpopular decisions. I really want to get things back on track with us. I hope that I also have your respect, because being a good parent to you is important, and I think respect is vital to healthy relationships, especially ours!" Sometimes our children just need a nudge to open up to us. Look for opportunities to discuss your relationship, especially if things are amuck! Children will usually respond.

Points to Remember

Respect is an essential component of Healthy Relationships. Respect for self and others is fundamental to good behaviour.

As parents, we need to help our children understand the value of respect; thus they need to live respect. Remember we are our children's most influential role models. Pay attention to how you show respect. Take your own pulse - how respectful you are has direct impact on how your children will behave. Treat those

Chapter Four • Respect

around you respectfully and expect the same back. It's an equation that works!

Respectful relationships are better able to recover from distress.

It's never too late to turn a conversation or relationship around. An apology, rewind, and replay can be very effective. Saying sorry, trying to say it differently, can be very helpful. Showing your child that respect is important will go a long way towards a more respectful, rewarding relationship! And more fun!

Remember Mommy and Daddy, little ears are listening!

"My child is not perfect - no more than I am – so we suit each other admirably."
Alexander Smith

Chapter Five

BEING PRESENT and Showing Up!

Another way to enhance the parenting experience is BEING MINDFUL, being PRESENT! We can spend a ton of time being AROUND our children, which can be very different than being WITH our children. Just like the parallel play displayed by very young children who play side by side without interacting with each other, parents can fall into the same pattern. As parents leading busy, often complicated lives, we are often distracted from the present. We get so distracted with the past – 'Did I really say that! Did I remember to call about that bill? etc. etc. - or with worry about the future – 'What will I cook for supper? I need to finish that file from work, after I do the dishes in the sink, and I better call and see how Mom is doing.' - that we are really not enjoying the moment right in the here and now with our children! What a waste, and we will regret it.

Life goes so quickly; it is so sad that when we actually have the time to share with our children, we are really absent. It is so easy for this to happen. It helps tremendously just to become aware of this issue and to turn our attention to it. With practice, it does improve. A good friend told me she reminds herself that life is full of firsts, which is especially true for children. The first time anyone experiences something, it can be quite extraordinary. The first Spelling Bee, the first Christmas concert, the first school dance, hockey tournament, are very exciting, almost palpable trembling! Don't miss out whenever you can, and when present, really be there, experience how they feel, put your finger on that pulse, and go with the beat. You'll likely enjoy the dance!

Be Focused, Be Organized

It also helps when we are organized. When we have time set aside for certain responsibilities, it allows our free time to be just that, to be free to be in the moment. Set aside a time of the day for planning. We all should spend some time planning the day and the week. Set time in the schedule for bill paying and mail sorting, household chores, reading, etc. These duties or activities don't have to take up a lot of time, but when done haphazardly over the day they can seem to be endless. Try getting up out of bed a little earlier than the children and you'll find you can achieve miracles in 30 minutes! Try assigning Thursday evenings just before or after supper, when everyone who's able helps out for 30 minutes with household chores. In a family of four, that's a combined effort of two hours of housework which will free you all up for more fun together on the weekend. It also teaches your children responsibility and respect for the house and your time maintaining it! So when you organize your day and week, you can better enjoy the down-time with your children or yourself. Try scheduling in "fun time" with the kids, a special supper, a picnic lunch. When we commit a plan to paper and share our idea with the family, we are more likely to follow through with it. Make time together a priority. It is easy to get distracted with day-to-day chores, and, if allowed, they can be consuming. Take control of your time and, with some planning, you'll get more done than you think and have some dedicated time and head space for the good stuff!

Enjoy the Regular

Being mindful, paying attention to the moment, allows us to actually enjoy the mundane, the regular, and the day-to-day. We can find much greater joy in a conversation with our partner or child if we are truly focused on the person and the content. How many times do we say, "I didn't hear that, say it again." It looked like we were listening! But we weren't. How often do we have to repeat things to other family members? Countless. So when you sit at the table for supper, which you should do daily with your family, try to be fully focused on the present. Get everyone to help prepare the table, sit down, and start eating together! I know this is challenging - I don't get seated until mid-meal unless I make it a mission and request the courtesy from other family members! See if you get more out of the experience by planning it and look for support around it. State that you think it is important that you all start the meal together, and that means everyone helping out. A calm, cohesive approach to meal time can provide a great opportunity for connecting with family and having fun. Once an idea is expressed, like, 'I really think meal time is a great time for us to connect and relax together, so let's work together to make meals special!', the idea gains momentum to becoming a reality. Soon candles are lit, fancy glasses are out and nickels are under plates. Fun can be found anywhere. As the parent, it is often necessary to express the explicit; be clear. By stating what is felt to be important, children can see the issue more clearly, as will your partner. Nobody can read minds, and what one may think is a universal understanding, another may not see as remotely important!

Chapter Five • Being Present and Showing Up

The next time you pick the kids up from an activity or school, take a few minutes to connect before you all rush into the next part of the day. Hold hands, have a hug, ask what was really good about their event and if anything went wrong. Make it your mission to listen intently and be present. You may then actually remember the next day that they invited four friends over for a "hockey sticks" match in your living room! Can you remember the last time you looked your child in the eye and asked them about their day, without doing anything else, like throwing on supper, pulling out of the school yard, emptying the dishwasher, etc.? We are often speaking to our children while doing something else. Try to sit still with your children for five minutes while chatting with them after you pick them up or get home from work. See how it feels. I think you'll like it! This exercise helps them and you to learn to be present, mindful, and attentive to the moment. Life is a series of moments. Enjoy them.

You will also feel a deeper connection with your children when you connect more intensely. It isn't magic; it just takes the resolve to do it. It will actually enhance all your relationships. Just remember how easy it was to do with that high school sweetheart, without any effort; you were locked on, engaged in every word. So you know you can do it; you just have to make it so! Practice and more practice and wow, you're doing it. You won't be perfect, but you'll BE PRESENT a whole lot more! This will reap many rewards in your relationships at home. Your partner and children will learn by example; they will appreciate your undivided attention and learn how it's done. Again, this will enhance their current and future relationships and ability to focus on the NOW.

We are very easily distracted from the present, right from the moment we awaken in the early morning. Our minds start racing fairly quickly, 'what day is it?', 'what do I have to do today?'

and so forth. In the morning just try to take a few moments to awaken slowly, listen to the birds chirping, enjoy the feel of your nice warm, comfortable bed, the stillness. Remember Barbara's suggestion about early morning prayer, meditation, spiritual reading. See if that helps set a better beginning to the day, a calmer approach. I review these issues with patients and families all the time. People who suffer from Anxiety are often terribly distracted with the past or future. This absolute waste of time is not only unnecessary, but destructive. So don't let the irrelevant become the focus. Let the current be important - it's really all we've got. Remind yourself of how wonderful it is to be alive, to have today; don't waste it. This point in time will never be ours again, so take the time to enjoy it, allow yourself the privilege to be focused, to be present, in the present!

Showing Up

The second point I'd like to address in this chapter is the concept of "Showing Up!" Even on our worst days at work, the hardest part is actually showing up. Dragging yourself up out of bed, getting to that dreaded boot camp class or the seemingly irrelevant breakfast meeting is the most difficult step. Once you get there, things usually fall into place. It's the same thing with the children. You've got to first show up in order to be present. Now we all can't be everywhere all the time, or maybe due to job commitments it's only a small amount of the time, but we've got to get to some stuff, especially the important stuff. Talk about balance! Of course there's the very important "You" time, but that usually doesn't take that much time to satisfy, since we're not too used to it yet. How often do you hear children talk about the one time you didn't make it to something important, versus the countless times you did make it. Showing up really matters, and they are noticing. Don't feel guilty when you can't make it; talk about why you can't get there and tell them you want to hear all about it when you see them. When children know that their parents are making effort and are interested, they are very reasonable. Children are the first ones to usually let us off the hook. Just be respectful of that and be honest. Children know after a while what the scoop is!

So be as involved as you can. Sometimes your involvement will be easier and more enjoyable than others. If you don't get involved for a particular reason, examine that reason and address it. Don't allow a fixable problem to interfere with your quality of life with your child. Take control of the situation. Self-reflect. Is it confidence, shyness, or poor planning? Do not get into the mind trap of not enough time; we know that it is all about priorizing. Addressing the issue will help you and your child tremendously. Don't compare yourself to others; only ever compare yourself to your former self. If being more involved in your child's life is important to you but you feel restrained in some way, look into yourself for the solution. It is there. So if you can reschedule a work meeting to attend a school event, do it. If you can be the team chaperone at the basketball tournament, do it. Coach your child's team, have a class party, help with the recycling program, look for an opportunity to be involved together, because soon they won't want you around as much. As hard as it is to believe, they grow out of us! At least if you've made them a high priority to you, there's a better chance you'll rank high with them too. And after the weekend tournament, or the house-altering class party, let the kids clean up and check yourself into the spa. There are always ways to find balance!

Points to Remember

Become more aware of actually being focused on the here and now. Being present enhances your experience.

Try not to be just in your child's presence, but actually be present in body, mind, and spirit!

Take time in the morning to connect and again when you see each other after school or work. Make your conversation with them the priority of the moment - sit down together, be close, be focused. Try to do this regularly and you will feel much better connected to each other.

Being aware of being present, mindful, and focused is the beginning. Practicing will help it get easier and more rewarding.

Remember, in order to be present, we actually have to be there! Don't forget to show up!

"If you surrender completely to the moments as they pass, you will live more richly those moments."
Anne Morrow Lindberg

Chapter Six

Communication

Communication begins the moment you enter a room.

How something is said can be way more powerful than what is actually said. The tone, body language, volume, setting, even timing, are all important factors. How and what is said can make it or break it! The intended message can get lost or amplified depending on the delivery. Many interpersonal disputes centre around the words used, the tone, the misinformation. Communication is central to connectedness, to relationships. Have you ever noticed your communication style? How it works for or against you? When you enter the house, do you call out a friendly 'hi' or a disgruntled silence? We all have a style; some people are more flexible than others, some more rigid, but most everyone can benefit from self-reflection. Communication skills can be improved, changed, and learned. All it takes is motivation! And then some practice!

Communication at Home

Communication with family members is likely much more challenging at times than communication with most other people. Often when we are dealing with our children or spouse about an issue of contention, we are quite emotionally charged. We may be frustrated, saddened, excited, worried, or experiencing countless other emotions. Once you add emotion into a conversation, things can really flare up. We often also don't pay a lot of attention to our communication at home. Of course we usually take our relationships at home for granted, and, unfortunately, this can lead to some neglect, and thus these relationships are not as good as they potentially could be. Our communication with family does need attention and care, and if we make the effort, it will have rewards!

Calm the Waters and Self-Reflect

The first thing to remember about good communication is to try to do it calmly! When emotions are flared, usually our tone is also, and things just don't go as we intended. It is difficult to wipe out all emotion from a conversation, nor do we want to. But we do need to be in control, and we are much more effective when the message is clear and not flavored with ineffective or destructive adjectives or disrespectful tones. The adjectives may be somewhat therapeutic for the one speaking; however, for the receiver, they become the focus, thus derailing the message completely and moving the conversation in an unintended direction.

So pay attention to how you are feeling at the onset; maybe say how you feel at the beginning of the conversation and then move on to the message, which may be about how you are feeling. So if you know from experience that your communication is not effective if you are emotionally charged up, and if you start off feeling angry or hurt or whatever, then try to calm the particular emotion(s). You could count to 100, go for a quick (or long!) walk, get a drink of water, hug the person first, (remind yourself you do love them!) or try any other calming technique that works for you. Slow, deep breathing is a powerful and effective way to help the body and mind calm down.

A suggested way of starting a conversation when you are revved up could be: "I really need to talk to you and I need you to know that I am really upset and hurt about what just happened! I am going to try to remain calm because I think this is a really important issue for us to discuss, and it's important because you are important to me..." Once you feel that the other person realizes that you are experiencing a particular emotion, you don't have to continue to try to convince them in the conversation. It is stated and dealt with; now move on to the message.

Plan it Out

Another point to consider in communication is to try to have a plan if it is about something important to you. For example, if you wanted to discuss with your spouse spending more time together, give the conversation some thought; think about what you want to achieve and the message you want to get across. Sometimes writing down your script and practicing beforehand can be helpful. Remember, communication skills can be refined through practice, so practice! A suggested script with your partner could be: "I've noticed that we don't really get that much time together anymore, and I miss that! I think that it's really important that we take care of our relationship. Even though we are faced with so many distractions, how do you think we could start making sure we have some couple time?" After you engage your partner, ask for input, make some of your own suggestions, and make a firm plan for your next date before you end the conversation. And have fun!

A Time and Place

Choosing the correct setting is another important part of planning. A particular conversation may be very appropriate in the bedroom but NOT in the kitchen. Sometimes it's really hard not to dive into a monologue you've been suppressing for three weeks, especially if you are tired, cranky, etc. But try to refrain from getting into something at the absolute wrong time; it won't be very effective and will most likely just make you feel bad. One thing that occurs frequently is parents reprimanding children in front of other people. This usually just makes that child feel humiliated in front of others, especially friends, and there is no message received! So if the issue needs immediate addressing, ask your child to come and help you with something in another private room, and discuss your concerns. Giving the conversation privacy will allow the message to be clear, as well as letting your child know you respect them. They will appreciate this courtesy. The same goes for comments to spouses, which may seem funny at the time in front of your dinner guests, but may actually be hurtful to your spouse. If you have something important to say to your partner or child, give it the correct setting or let it go for now.

Clarify, Clarify

When you are conversing with a family member or anyone else, don't hesitate to ask for clarification. State what you think is the gist of the conversation or message and ask if you've gotten it right. This can be effective even with young children and can be vital with teens and spouses! Also summarize what you are saying to be sure your message is clear! These techniques could sound like this: "Ok, so I want to make sure I fully understand what you are saying to me because it's important to me to get it right! So you are saying that......Is that correct, do I have that right?" Be careful to say this respectfully, without a hint of sarcasm. And to make yourself clear, try this: "I want to summarize what I am saying to make sure it's clear, since we've talked about so much, and I really want my message to get across! So what I am saying is.....Do you have any questions? Is what I'm saying making sense to you?"

Have a Follow-up Plan

Have a plan when you are concluding a conversation. Don't leave things hanging! So when you discuss with your daughter that you are concerned about how much time she is spending on MSN and you never get to see her alone anymore, make a plan for lunch for the next day. Have a follow-up plan to maybe revisit the issue in three day's time for reassessment.

That may sound like this: "I know you really love being in contact with your friends, but I am afraid that the computer is taking up too much of your time and I really miss having time with you! I think having balance in your life is really important! So why don't we look at how much time you are spending on all your activities and see if some rebalancing is due! We could do the same for me too! Why don't we start with having lunch together tomorrow at your favorite restaurant! Next time we go out we could invite a friend too. Is that okay with you? It's really important to me to spend some time with you! Why don't we try to check in with each other once a week on this issue to make sure we keep on top of things?" Then go directly to the kitchen calendar (a must-have for organization) and pencil in the lunch and the weekly check-ins. Remember, organization is critical!

Being Respectful

Another key to successful communication is respect. Respecting the person you are communicating with ensures the integrity of the conversation. And remember, it is never too late to turn things around in a conversation; as soon as you realize things are not going as you intended, just say so and try again. If you feel you are not up to the conversation, try to defer it. This is fine so long as you don't continually put things off! Also give your family the same luxury; if your son just isn't up to discussing his academic future on a Friday night, give him some slack and plan another time suitable to both of you. Again, there is a right time and place for a particular conversation.

A good way of turning things around in a conversation could be: "This conversation is not going as I planned. I'm sorry for sounding so mad. Really, I'm feeling hurt. What I really wanted to say was....." or, "It sounds like you're kind of upset right now and the message is getting a bit mixed up. Why don't we take a break and try again later?" We can always apologize after the fact as well, but this will only work so often. Remember, if we imagine someone we respect outside our family is watching our interaction, that may also keep us on our toes! Keep it real, sincere, and if you say what you really mean, with a respectful tone, you will get your message across.

Create Opportunities

As parents, we need to create many opportunities for communication with our family. Very easily we can all be occupying our own separate 20 square feet and only communicate on vital issues such as, "Mom, can you get me something to eat?" or, "Can I have a ride?" or, " Honey, where are my socks?"! So we need to have rituals that we stick to in order to ensure regular, vital, contact and communication. One suggestion I make to families is to ensure you have supper together almost always. No matter how small, simple, or fast this meal may have to be, it should be together. Everyone has to eat, and it is an opportunity for family members to connect on how the day was, anything exciting going on, what's next on the agenda, and so on. It is also very important nutritionally!

If we don't create lots of times to talk, we won't. Our children need to feel at ease discussing the mundane in order to feel able to broach the trickier topics. Many families don't share meal times; it is easy to get into that habit with differing schedules. Sometimes grabbing a pizza together for a quick park picnic before soccer is a great idea. Pizza is half healthy, and the picnic gets you together! Be creative. Have your children help with meal preparation. No mater what age, most can help with something - setting the table, helping with the baby, or possibly assisting with cooking. It helps them share in the ceremony and see the importance of sitting and enjoying the meal together no matter how simple the meal may be.

Another way to ensure some time together with each child is to devote at least 15-30 minutes at the end of each day for one-on-one activity. Story time, game time, or just talk time are all good ideas. It is good for both of you and provides an opportunity for issues to arise. If we aren't sitting at the table, we can't be served. If we don't allow ourselves to be available to our children, they are much less likely to approach us on an issue, big or small. You may even have to play PS3 to get your point across that you want to spend time together! So make sure you show them, not just tell them, that you are there for them because they may get tired of looking for you!

After school is a great time to connect if you are able. Try to have a conversation, even if brief, before the mad dash for the TV, computer, or swim meet. Give them a hug, ask about their day, and see if they need anything addressed. Be attentive and interested, and they are more likely to let you into their world. You don't have to be controlling or interfering, just interested.

Ask if they are looking for advice. Younger children will need more direction than teens of course. Our parenting is an ongoing, evolving process. The more we are involved, the more there is to communicate about and help our children navigate through.

Communication with Your Partner

Contact with partners is also an area in need of attention. Make sure you communicate about the children. Talk about your goals for them, your concerns, and how to best parent them. Ask each other how you think you are doing in the area of communication. Think about their input and self reflect. Communicate with your partner about your relationship. How is communication between you? Do you have enough time together? How can things get even better? Talking will keep things going and growing, and that is only a good thing!

Sometimes couples get stuck in old communication styles which don't really nurture their relationship. Partners can get into a certain pattern of body language, tone, gestures, and phrases that may not be particularly helpful and may be actually harmful. Have you ever had a family or couple vacation where things were great, communication was easy, people were calm, respectful, and there was a lot of fun, and then after five minutes (or less!) back in the house, the old patterns of togetherness re-emerge? Old habits can be tough to break, and it is amazing how stuck into patterns of relating to others we can get.

Trying to recognize if this is an issue for you and your partner is the first step. Step two is actually raising it in discussion, as a point of interest. It could sound something like this: "I would like to take a few minutes to discuss something with you! (smile, be

Chapter Six • Communication

warm and non-threatening) I have noticed lately that we seem to get into a pattern of communicating that ends up with us arguing. I would really like it if we could try to change the way we are communicating, to try to be more clear and direct, while being respectful of each other. What do you think about that? Do you have any suggestions of what may work better for us?"

Keep in mind the points about communication in general raised earlier. Have a plan of what you want to say and achieve, be calm, respectful, choose the right time and place so both of you are comfortable, and make a follow-up plan, like " ...OK this is great! Why don't we really try to practice these things, and let's make plans for a nice supper out on Saturday and review how we are doing?" Also remember that if what you are trying to say is going all wrong, it is perfectly fine to stop and start from the beginning. Perhaps by keeping these pointers in mind, your communication with your partner and other significant people in your life may become inspirational to the little ones watching very, very closely! If your partner is struggling with issues of communication, lead by example, and you will likely see results.

Always remember that your children are watching very closely how you communicate with the world. They see how you speak to them, to your spouse, friends, neighbours, teachers, the grocery clerk, your mother, mother in-law, siblings, everybody. They learn the most about communication from you. They will reflect this learning in their communication, in their modeling of you. I always marvel over what I call the inappropriate shadowing phenomenon. You are sitting at the dinner table with guests, and your eight year-old makes a comment at the table that he has heard you say many times, but it sounds extremely inappropriate from him, especially at the wrong place and time! Your little fellow was only trying to be funny, and heck, it sounded funny when

Inspired Parenting

you said it. You laughed your head off (even if others didn't, he's really only watching you!). So make it a great opportunity to educate your child, in private of course, after he apologizes to your guest. Then self-reflect, please, on really how appropriate that comment is when you do use it. If it didn't sound good out of the mouth of your babe, well....Take the time to explain context to your child, explain how things may sound to others. Your child may say something with a completely different goal or intent than what gets across to others. An example of this is when children are trying to learn how to use humor or sarcasm. Help them; teach them how to navigate through these challenges. Remember, they need your direction!

Chapter Six • Communication

Points to Remember

How we communicate is as important as what we are communicating.

Self reflection is an important step in making our own progress with communication.

Communication is a skill that can be learned and modified... Motivation necessary!

Things to remember when communicating:
- Choose the right setting and time.
- Attempt to be as calm as possible if you are upset!
- Body language counts.
- Tone sets the tone.
- Plan what you want to say.
- Have a follow up plan to effectualize what you just talked about, what's next?
- Respect is key.
- Try to be calm!!!!!!!!!!!!!!!!!!
- Practice, it helps.
- Stop, rewind, and replay allowed!

"I looked at my child twice and then he was present to me."
Fr.JJM

Chapter Seven

Unplug Your Kids! I think there should be huge Billboards with this on it!

Technology today is amazing! Advances in the IT world are helping in many aspects of our world such as travel, medical research, and many more areas, as well as communication! How is this new age of computers affecting your world? More importantly, how is it affecting your child's world? Most likely when a child or teen logs onto the computer, it isn't to research the latest NASA advancements, but rather to play the latest game or communicate with peers. Unfortunately, I know many children in my practice who are playing video games for six to eight hours a day on weekdays and even more on weekends! That is more than a full time job! Children get home from school, supervised or not, log on at 3:00 pm and get off for supper, then get back on until bedtime!

Children are exposed to the world of video games from a very early age. Many toys designed for young children have associated internet web pages and games. Many television shows for children, starting again at young ages, have web sites for games. So pre-schoolers are introduced to gaming very quickly, and very innocently parents go along with it. Video game sites normalize gaming, stating that 99% of teens are playing video games. Unfortunately, this statistic is likely close to accurate, given my experience. So, video games are introduced early, normalized, romanticized, and promoted by the media and often by parents and certainly peers. Wow, that's a lot of momentum in one direction! Can you think of any other activity that boasts that over 90% of a particular age group are active participants? Ninety percent of children are not physically active, reading regularly, in band, or in drama, etc., etc.! How many children/teens spend equal screen time to reading time? Not too many I see in my office are reaching that ratio.

Cell phone texting. Could that qualify as an epidemic yet? It is incredible how many nonrelevant, useless interchanges occur daily. Most parents will purchase the unlimited texting package with the cell phone or else pay hundreds of dollars monthly on this option. Lots of teens tell me they send/receive over 400 texts a day! That is an enormous amount of time, distraction, and emotional energy! Can you think of one other activity someone would or could do more than that? Breathe maybe! Some will argue that texting has a role in the current generation of youth for social connectedness. I can see this in some situations, when done in moderation. Also, it can be great when your child is looking for you and is trying to discreetly ask you to come get them from a wild party! So as with most things, texting can have its place too, but also like most things, moderation is key!!

Be Informed

As parents, I think we let this crazy situation creep up on us because we are not really aware of the potentially addictive quality of these activities. Hand-held video games, even cell phones, are addictive with texting and games. Our children are bombarded with these devices with very few limitations. Younger children like to play games, and teens like to communicate with friends. So when we give them the means to do these favourite activities with no limits, it should not be surprising what happens! When the Internet is added to the mix, children's boundaries can be completely lost. Through some Internet communications, face-to-face contact is not a factor, and thus boundaries are easily lost. The limitless access to information, through the Internet, some of which should not be tapped into, can also be very influential.

As a society we have given our children the keys to the world and then gone out for supper! They desperately need direction and boundaries. When children can escape into the video world, some are more vulnerable than others to wanting to stay there. Face-to-face interaction with peers is where our children learn real communication, but it is a lot easier to communicate via internet. The lack of the face-to-face interaction eliminates a lot of anxiety and unfortunately dissolves a lot of common courtesy and communication etiquette. People are more readily able to cross boundaries when talking to a screen. Things are said on screens that would be much more intimidating to say in person. There are no immediate consequences. Bullying is easy in cyberspace. Social slights in-person are easy enough; on screen it is even easier. Just being left out is very hurtful.

Tremendous education needs to happen. We as parents need to be educated, and we must educate our children. Find out what they are doing on the computer, investigate it, and learn about it. Also keep in mind your child's developmental and cognitive abilities. Are they capable of navigating through communication on the Internet? Do they understand the permanency of putting things in print or in pictures? Most children and teens do not fully appreciate the implications and subtleties of these technological activities and have to be educated about them. And of course they think that all their friends are doing it, so there can't be anything wrong with it! Of course, there is huge benefit from the Internet, in many, many ways. It is certainly the way of the present and the future, and thus as parents we must get savvy! Get savvy so you have authority on the issue and can not only be policing, but also helpful!

Be Directive

You need to give your children limits on what they can use and for how long. Put limits in at the beginning; we all know it is much more difficult to 'claw back' than to move forward. Do not use these devices as a babysitter that keeps them quiet or you will eventually regret that. Make sure they ask permission before using these devices so you know when they started. I recommend that children do not use video games on weekdays and use them on weekends under supervision for a reasonable time; maybe two half-hour stints is enough. To many people, that sounds very strict, but it can work, and you can be sure they will squeeze a bit more time out of you anyway!

Caution! If your child has been allowed to build up his/her time on the 'screen' to an amount you now disagree with, being supportive and withdrawing this time gradually may be necessary. For some children, they have built their world around these games or the computer or both. You need to help them rebalance with your support and guidance. Remember, they didn't do this without consent. Help substitute other activities; don't just leave them hanging. For the time they are gaming or chatting, they are not learning other ways to socialize or entertain themselves. Reading can be a great pastime, and they should start early. Every hour on screen should be matched to an hour of reading. This suggestion often shocks children and parents alike in my office! Be creative in hooking in your young reader, and be directive. Make it a priority, and it just might happen.

Get yourself educated and stay informed. You may need to consider delaying the use of the Internet for certain things until you think they can handle it - that may be at least late junior high for independent communication via the Internet. They need to be able to keep conversations clear and stay out of trouble. They need you to sometimes look at conversations or review what they said. Tell them you respect their privacy but at least starting off you will need to monitor them a bit. If you start off with openness about it, they will accept it better. It also allows them to realize that anyone can see what they are writing, not just the intended audience. Just as you can look on, so can other people at the receiving end. So many teens and even adults post pictures on the Internet that can be easily misinterpreted! From a more extreme perspective, court cases can be won or lost over pictures on the net! There are consequences of irresponsible behaviour, and once something is written or posted on the web, it has much more far reaching effects than a simple conversation between two people. This is an important point that parents need to be aware of and need to educate their children about. Don't be complacent. Smart children can make bad decisions; help them be savvy about these issues!

Many children come into my office playing their hand-held video game device; they walk around with it, they try to speak with it on, and they play with friends with it. Actually, a lot of socializing goes on around video games. Online games are common, so kids actually think they are socializing while doing this! Some children tell me they play with 'friends'; upon questioning you realize that these 'friends' are actually just on-line acquaintances. Classrooms are full of teens texting one another, two rows apart! Many teens sitting at a restaurant are usually texting, not chatting, with Mom and Dad. Ask them to put the phone down while you are socializing; make the most of your time together. This teaches them respect for those whom they are with, and helps them set boundaries for themselves. It will enhance their awareness of being present, being polite, and help them enjoy who they are with at the time! Take advantage of these teachable years, because before you know it, they will be texting you from college for more funds!

Skills Building

For children with true Anxiety, especially Social Anxiety, the computer can be very helpful in initiating social contacts. In this age of Chat Rooms and Internet, our children can meet a ton of people with common interests, and friendships can develop. But this needs close supervision and education. We are all aware of the dangers of sexual predators on the Internet, and children who don't have a strong social network are more vulnerable to being drawn into cyberspace relationships.

Just as the screen is easier for most people to 'talk' to, it is infinitely easier for someone with Anxiety to communicate with peers via a 'screen'. However, if used excessively, the computer or texting may become the only form of effective communication for that child, and he/she does not develop any confidence in real life, face-to-face social interactions. I know lots of children who can text or use the Internet no problem, but find it tremendously difficult to pick up the telephone and call the same person and say the same thing in-person! Their anxiety is so strong that their confidence in social interactions, especially any interactions involving perceived risk of rejection, is in their boots. So it is easier to be turned down on an invitation online, in text, than face-to-face, where their disappointment can be seen. So if you have a child who is anxious about social interactions and needs help getting things started, please help them. Make suggestions; ask if you can help in any way. The computer may be of some assistance, but don't let it become the only form of communication.

Encourage the use of the home telephone, from a young age, so you can monitor and give feedback as to how they are doing communicating on the telephone. Give suggested scripts when they have to call someone, and make opportunities for them to call people. Ask them to call and order the pizza or check to see if their movie is in stock. It is an important skill for them to learn, and you should be the one to teach them! If your child has enough trouble with social anxiety that it is visible to you, it is probably pretty high, and they should likely see a professional about it. But even children without Anxiety are becoming quite computer dependant and need us to sometimes force them off screen and into the real world of face-to-face, voice-to-voice contact. They would likely benefit greatly by you just pulling the plug for a while and going for a walk in the woods! Being in the woods, close to nature, is actually really important for all of us. I think it helps us get grounded and feel connected to nature, which is very therapeutic. Try it yourself and find out just how great it is to jump off your email and go for a walk! That reminds me, I'm due my dose of beating the trail; see ya later! Don't forget to monitor your own computer use! A lot of parents are on the computer way too much, or text during supper out with the family! Screen etiquette is important for everyone. Remember, we lead by example. Another good reason for me to get off this computer!!

Suggested Scripts

Your child may be confused if out of the blue you start limiting their gaming time or cell phone usage. It's important to ask them how they think gaming/computer or texting is affecting them. Some

Chapter Seven • Unplug Your Kids

children are more insightful than others. Many kids in my practice very openly say that gaming takes up lots of time, and, even when they are not gaming, they are thinking about the game, even in school. Many teens in my office are texting until I ask them to put it away, and then they usually do. Our children see these activities as normal like breathing. Express your concern, if you have one, about their screen time. A conversation with a younger child could sound like this: "I/we have noticed that you are playing your video game a lot lately, are you enjoying it? I wonder if you think about the game much when you are not playing it? I really feel that we need to rethink about how much time you are gaming, because when you are gaming you are missing out on other activities (anyone can only do one thing at a time), which I feel are important for you, like reading, playing with friends, playing outdoors, being with family. I know I really miss reading with you. So let's make a plan of how we can cut the gaming down a bit and start doing a few different things. What other things would you like to do? I know you used to love..." Some children will protest a little, some a lot. That's OK, you are the boss here, and it's not really a democracy, yet! As the parent, you need to follow through with your plan. Once you make this a priority, things will change. Your child needs you to follow through; they cannot do this alone. Remember, you allowed the situation to evolve; now you must be part of the solution.

Concerns about your teen being over-invested in the 'screen' could sound like this: "I/We have noticed recently that the 'screen' time is really building, and I actually counted the other day that you were on the computer for 5 hours! Do you think that is routine for you now? I know that it's really easy for 'screen time' to build up, and that it's an easy way to communicate with your friends, but I am really concerned that it is cutting into some real social interactions, let alone studying, exercise, and family time. It may be hard for you to fully appreciate the value of a balanced day, but it is really important. I want you to be healthy and I think we need to look at this. Let's look at how we can rebalance and set a specific time in the day, after a few other things are accomplished, for screen time. What do you think? I'd also like to chat about how things are going with the Internet communication, any concerns there? Bullying can easily happen via the Internet, does that ever happen to you? Also a lot of 'chat rooms' are inappropriate and I know you can be exposed to a lot of "everything" on the net. How are you doing with this?"

It is important for parents to be interested and involved with their teens with respect to these issues. Parents also need to ask direct questions. They of course will think they know a lot more about these issues than you; they will likely know more about the devices and programs, but they definitely need guidance with appropriate usage and the implications of some of these issues. For example, Internet pornography is now a problem; make sure you know if it is an issue for your child. They are still kids and vulnerable to the pull of the screen, not unlike many adults in fact. Remember, you are still in control of the computer. It's still not a full democracy, and parenting requires tough decisions sometimes. Be respectful and communicate clearly. The message will be more clear and better heard.

Points to Remember

Become very aware of what your child is doing onscreen. Take an

Chapter Seven • Unplug Your Kids

accurate account of how much time your child is spending on their games, phone, computer, and even television. If you cannot answer this question, you need to. Are you on-line a bit too much?

Lots of children can build up to eight hours a day on a screen. That's as many hours as many people work in a day! And get paid!

Screens can become addictive and addicts think about the game as much off screen as on.

Start from the beginning by limiting usage. Always emphasize that the gadgets are privileges you pay for, literally, and earn. By being directive and setting limits from the beginning, you don't have to take back so much. Limit how long and when your children can access these activities.

Become educated and educate your child. Knowledge is power.

Evaluate your own screen time. You should be exercising for more time than you are playing on a screen. At least by playing with a ball you are having fun and helping your heart!

Be supportive if your child has found themselves a little overindulged in the screen scene. They will need your guidance and support!

> *"At ten my mother made me read a book. Now at fifteen I am reading Dickens."*
> *Fr. JJM*

Chapter Eight

When Your Child Is Not Succeeding

I have one of the greatest jobs in the world: I get to help children reach their potential, to help them be happy and healthy. It is extremely rewarding to see patients overcome challenges. Working with children and their families, bringing up my own children and experiencing their trials and accomplishments, has helped me see how sincere children are. They are who they are; no fooling, it's just all out there!

What I have found universal to all of these children is that they all want to be successful - successful with friends, school, family, sports, or other activities. Some areas will be more important to some than others, but they all want to do well, to please, to be accepted, and valued. I have never met a child who didn't want to succeed. So if your child is struggling with something important, it's not because they want to!

Acceptance

One of the first things we must do as parents is to recognize who our children really are, what their strengths are, and their areas of need.

Chapter Eight • When Your Child Is Not Succeeding

We need to help potentiate their strengths, channel their efforts, and aim to understand their needs. Accepting our children for who they are isn't always easy. As soon as we anticipate becoming parents, we start creating an image of our children, our expectations. An athlete, a scholar, a musician, it's hard to resist envisioning something to which we want them to aspire. What arrives from Father Genetics and is then sculpted from our family and societal environment, however, may be something quite unexpected! It could still be great, just different from what we thought!

But we must remember, except for some occasional genetic twist of fate, adoption or blended family, that our children are a biological extension of us. Just as it can be difficult for us to see similarities in appearance between ourselves and our children while others can see it clearly, the same can be true for behavioural and emotional traits. The apple doesn't usually fall too far from the tree. You may have to shine up a few rough spots, but the apple is still the apple, and you are the tree. So don't look too far out of the orchard when you start wondering, "where did we get that kid!" You are the major determinants of who you have before you, genetically and environmentally, unmistakably!

Be the Detective

And remember, children want to be well-adjusted, "popular", academically strong, talented at their game, organized, and held in high esteem by all. So if they are really struggling in an area, it is not because they are trying to drive you crazy, looking to defy you, or desiring to make you wish you were reading about "Childless Couples"! If a child is struggling in a particular area, they probably have something going on, and you should try to figure it out. You know your child better than anyone else, so trust your instincts! If you feel something is not right, then you are probably correct. You are the one doing homework with them (or should be) and putting them to bed. You see how they interact with you and others; you have your finger on their pulse. So don't [just] rely on others to identify issues. You have to take the lead in this whenever possible. You are your child's biggest and best advocate. Be there for them, especially in their area of need.

The School Factor

Many issues of concern don't become apparent until school starts, sometimes preschool. This is when children are expected to socialize with other children and learn to conform to social norms and expectations. They have to adjust to new authorities, and sometimes this is very difficult, depending on the level of discipline at home. So for the first time, a child is interfacing with the world using the skills their parents have taught them. How does the outside world compare to their world at home? How flexible is the child in adapting to his or her new world with its different set of expectations? This can be a bigger adjustment for some than others. Even children who have attended day care for several years will find it different going into the more structured classroom environment. Once academic demands increase, learning difficulties may then become apparent.

Most children will, however, do just great! They will all have some area of minor challenge, but if there seems to be a consistent area of concern, look a little closer. Ask for collateral information; don't just wait for someone to speak up. For example, if the issue appears to be school-based, ask the teacher his or her opinion. Ask how your child compares to the average on that particular issue, and if they, as a professional, have any concerns. Request updates and communicate regularly if the issue is persisting. If you continue to see that there is an issue and the teacher does not, trust

Chapter Eight • When Your Child Is Not Succeeding

your instincts. Teachers will have different sets of experiences and levels of tolerance. Maybe you need to meet with the guidance counselor or principal. Make sure you pursue your concerns before they become major problems. A learning disability can become evident initially at home, with parents first noticing that certain concepts are grasped very slowly or have to be re-taught at home.

The teacher may or may not see things as early as you do as you are doing homework one-on-one, giving you a closer look at your child's step-by-step processing of the information. Homework should take a very short time in primary grades and even elementary. If it is taking your child an hour to get through 10-15 minutes of work, that's a good indication that something is not as it should be. Ask the teacher how long a task should take, and compare that to your child's time frame. All children are different, but there are basic guidelines that are usually quite accurate. Attention span is also important. Your child should be able to stay focused on their homework without too much hassle from you. If he or she is consistently looking for a pencil, a drink of water, going to the bathroom, or in general seems to be easily distracted from the task at hand, that should be watched closely. If it persists, it needs further assessment.

Possible Issues

The two major issues that interfere with learning in children are specific Learning Disabilities and Attention Deficit Hyperactivity Disorder, or ADHD. Many parents are very reluctant to explore the possibility of ADHD. They are afraid of stigma, labeling and the treatments. What many parents don't realize is that it is not the diagnosis that labels children, it is their behaviours. When a child cannot listen long enough to absorb the class material, to learn new concepts, and to illustrate what they have learned, that is what begins to define them or it is the other behavioural aspects of the condition. I'll review this medical condition in more detail in a later chapter.

What is really important to remember is that your child is likely doing their best. If your child is inattentive, distractible, or not learning, it's not because he or she loves being told 25 times to sit and do the worksheet. It's because he or she simply can't do it. It is very demoralizing to be told in class over and over again in front of peers to do better, to stop daydreaming or interrupting. It is really no fun falling behind the other students, and especially no picnic having to try to explain to Mom and Dad why they are not succeeding. They don't really know why they don't pay attention well. So you have to find out. These issues don't usually get better on their own and usually start to progress. Marks often get worse; concepts don't get learned as well as they should, and a self concept of being "stupid" can develop.

If school can help develop a love of or at least a positive attitude toward learning, then our child has already succeeded. It is pretty hard to love learning when it's as difficult as learning French from a Russian class! Unfortunately, a child can become pretty discouraged from learning when it is always so challenging, and he or she may ultimately give up. Many children who do not get the help they need have a greater risk of dropping out of school. That wasn't as big a deal 20 years ago, but it sure has impact now. You may find that you were able to buffer the work load from school by helping out in the younger grades, but then in Junior High, when students are expected to be more independent in class and don't want as much supervision and help from home, things start to fall apart academically or at least start to show signs of deterioration.

Chapter Eight • When Your Child Is Not Succeeding

I see a lot of good students with mild to moderate attention or learning difficulties who did well in elementary school because of good home support, but start to struggle more with the issues as they progress in school due to decreased structure and increased demands in the classroom. Lots of teens ask for help because they see these issues as preventing them from progressing, and they want help! Children and teens are often not afraid to ask for help. If you were struggling with the same issue, you would likely seek a resolution, and so you should afford your children the same right. It's usually parents, the ones without the symptoms, who are caught up in the stigma, thus preventing accurate diagnosis and treatment, instead of the symptomatic, suffering child! What does that say! Fear is sometimes our biggest impediment.

Look to Others

We are often fairly defensive about our children, and that is to be expected. Don't allow this protectiveness, however, to blind you to important insights that can help improve your child's life. Just as you would want the open-mindedness of your child's teacher to entertain your concerns, also be open to concerns brought to you. If a teacher is bringing up a concern, there is usually something to it. It takes a lot, in my experience, for concerns in the classroom regarding learning, attention, anxiety, or socializing to prompt the teacher into acting on it and bringing it to your attention. As you know, the average teacher has a broad spectrum of 'normal' to compare to, so if they have concerns, they are usually legitimate. They are reporting the issues to you; you need to explore what they mean.

The teacher is not usually just looking for a label. Many parents can become quite convinced the teacher is just trying to label a child to make their life [the teacher's] easier. That rarely happens;

it is your child and you who will truly benefit when the issue is explored and rectified. Concerns usually come from the school a bit later than ideal or not at all if your child is quiet and not disrupting others. A quiet child daydreaming, not learning to their potential but not bothersome, doesn't easily reach the teacher's radar. So don't dismiss concerns, investigate them. It could save you and your child a lot of grief!

The other issues to be aware of, aside from those in the academic arena, are the emotional, and social issues. Unfortunately, in today's society, our children can be exposed to many stressors, as well as conveniences. Anxiety in children is a real issue which can interfere with normal development. I'll explore Anxiety Disorders in a later chapter, but will begin here with a discussion of the more common, yet still very concerning issues. Again, children want to be socially comfortable - to have friends, be included and have fun. If that's not happening, look a little closer. Sometimes small issues, if addressed, can resolve a lot! Talk to your child, ask what they think. Ask them if they would like more friends and if they feel supported by their friends. If they feel rejected, ask them what they think might be the issue. They may not have any answers, but you will have started the dialogue.

In my experience with my patients, children can usually identify the issues quite well. They experience them and often see the pattern. They just need some support to discuss them. If a child is not socializing easily, if there are persistent issues of conflict with peers, feelings of rejection, incidents of oppositional behaviour, there may be something going on that needs further looking into. Impulsiveness in a child can lead to them being rejected by peers. Their behaviour may just be a little irritating and if persistent, over time may lead to peer issues. Feelings of rejection can then lead to a child becoming defensive and oppositional. You can see how

Chapter Eight • When Your Child Is Not Succeeding

a domino effect can easily and unintentionally evolve, with very destructive results for a child. These issues, if occurring, need your attention!

Ask the teacher for his or her observations. Discuss things with your spouse, friends, and parents. Sometimes we are too close to the situation to see what others do. Remember to stay open minded and not defensive. This is not easy to do, so ask choice people, people you trust. Observe your child in different settings. Having friends over is a great way to see for yourself the dynamic of the group and how your child interacts. You then can reflect together about how things went. This can work for young and older children. Get involved and see what's happening. Don't become so overpowering that your child feels you are intrusive. Be supportive, explore issues, and don't make assumptions about your child or the situation that will invalidate you to them.

A suggested script if you are concerned about how your child interacts with peers (perhaps you find him a bit too bossy): "George I am so glad you had your friends over. I think it went really well! What do you think was the best part? Do you think anything could have been better? I did notice a couple of times that you kind of like to be the boss. That's okay sometimes, but everyone should have a chance to lead the group and have their ideas heard. How do you think you could do that better?" Be supportive, and look for solutions together. Your child will listen to you. Make a plan of how to remind him of what to do the next time his friends are over! Sometimes a code word works well: "When Mom says pizza, it means you need to let someone else have the chance be the leader for a change!" We are the ones closest to our children to make the suggestions. Be thoughtful, respectful, and creative. Your child will surely benefit!

There are a number of concerns we may have about our children. Don't ignore your inner voice; pay attention to that persistent concern you have. We need to have confidence in our ability to know when something is not quite right. Don't allow apathy to win out. After you have explored issues and feel things are okay, move on. Don't create issues where there are none; just be attentive. You don't have to be Sherlock Holmes, just a caring parent who listens to her child and herself.

Bullying!

A big concern we all have as parents is Bullying! This can happen in so many ways, some I'm sure we haven't even fully recognized. It is heartbreaking to find out your child is being victimized in any way. Our children should be respected by others, attend school, activities, and participate in their life without harassment, prejudice, or intimidation. Unfortunately this doesn't always happen. Sometimes the torment, the ostracizing, comes from the most unlikely sources. A best friend who turned a corner, a jealous classmate, the school bully. Maybe the teasing is coming through texting or Internet communications.

The computer has revolutionized bullying. We hear about more violent crimes now by female teens; our children are exposed to so much more aggression than their predecessors. Media is very "out there", and music videos are often very explicit. Sexuality is expressed everywhere. Our children are faced with many more adult issues than we were. Boundaries are blurred, so be alert. Our children could be shunned or possibly outright harassed by a 'friend' on the Internet or through texting. Open communication helps here, so keep talking about these issues.

Chapter Eight • When Your Child Is Not Succeeding

Teaching your child about respect plays a big role in teaching them to reject bullying. A child who is respectful and expects respect back from others will be more likely to reject disrespect. Being aware and involved allows you to observe some of this stuff. Advocating for your child and teaching them how to self-advocate will help resolve it! This is an important issue that demands our attention. Ask about it regularly. You cannot change others. You cannot make schools deal with it the way you may want them to, but you can help your child learn to deal with this ugly human behaviour called bullying. You must help them learn to keep others' acceptance or rejection of them in perspective. You can help them learn that those who victimize are the ones with the problem, not the victim. This is tough to learn when children spend a lot of emotional energy trying to belong. They need tremendous support through these issues, so stay on top of things.

What Do You Do Next

Okay, so you've spotted a problem and you want to look closer. How do you do that? If the issue appears school-based, start there. Teachers, guidance counselors, and principals can all help. If there is an achievement issue with the school curriculum, a learning disability needs to be ruled out. Very smart children can still have a learning disability (LD) in any number of areas, such as Reading, Math Calculation, Math Reasoning, Written Expression, or Oral Expression. An LD can have significant impact on a child and their ability to master the curriculum. Schools are usually responsible for getting Educational Assessments done on children when indicated. The wait list for this can be very lengthy, however, so for those with private health insurance, sometimes a private psychologist is the way to go. The assessment should be thorough and assess for intelligence as well as possible learning disabilities. Knowing what is happening is an essential first step! If you feel the school is not on the same page as you, consult with your family doctor. He or she likely has a good sense of you and your family and is a good place to start when looking into childhood medical or behavioural issues. Your doctor may then assess for certain conditions and also discuss referring for further assessment by a psychologist or psychiatrist. If you feel the issue needs exploring, say so. Ask for a referral if you feel your child needs to see someone else and your family doctor does not make that suggestion.

Don't be shy asking for your child to be assessed. If your child had diabetes, you would request that they see a specialist for that. Emotional or behavioural issues are equally important and may arise from a medical condition that needs to be accurately diagnosed and treated. It is amazing to see how incredibly better a child can do once correctly diagnosed and treated. Chaos and torment can transform to happiness and health. When a child suffers from a behavioural or emotional medical condition, the child suffers significantly and so can the family. We can become very desensitized to certain behaviours in each other and accept them as 'normal'. But there is nothing normal about an unhappy, dysfunctional child or family.

It is extremely rewarding to see a child move away from being unhappy, unsuccessful, and tormented to good health. Look for answers. I see families all the time that had asked for help years previously or were told by teachers years ago that there were concerns, but things just didn't happen for them. Many years can pass and the problems can build up. It is not without consequences when real issues don't get addressed - consequences that may shape their lives and yours. So pay attention, ask questions, and search for help and answers that satisfy you and your child.

Chapter Eight • When Your Child Is Not Succeeding

Don't Overshoot It!

Do not confuse the issue of helping your child reach their potential with Overachieving. There can be as much grief with overachieving as underachieving. Our society is dangerously moving toward the completely overstuffed day. Just as materialism is becoming overwhelming, so are the activity demands on our children! There seems to be a sense among many parents that children have to be involved in something every night and weekend, that they must attend every lesson or practice, no matter what the price.

Hang around minor hockey parents for a while and count how many seconds it takes for the NHL to come up! I call minor hockey the Twilight Zone. Being just recently introduced to this world, I have had much to learn. This experience could be a whole other book! Many of these young children are in four to five different leagues, practices, associations - it is amazing. No wonder they get stress injuries; if their knees are hurting, imagine how their brain feels! I am a very strong supporter of physical activity for children. I think it is essential, but it too must be kept in check.

Structured activity is definitely good for children. They learn social skills, self-awareness, self-control, and many other skills. However, children can burn out too; they need down time, play time, and rest. These things are important, but often undervalued in our competitive, bustling society. Helping our children overcome their challenges may include helping them achieve balance and respect for their need for personal time.

Points to Remember

All children want to succeed! If your child is not succeeding academically, emotionally, or socially, find out why!

Recognize and appreciate who your child is. Understand and accept their strengths and needs. Work with them to reach their potential.

Our children are extensions of us. We must own up to the ownership!

When something is amuck, dig in and try to solve the issues.

Get collateral information. Have an open mind, and lose the stigma attitude, where applicable!!

Don't forget, have fun and enjoy the journey!!

"Problems are like festers – they need to be treated."
Fr. JJM

Chapter Nine

If I Were Principal for a Day!

Most administrative jobs look easier than they really are. Administrators usually have many people to keep happy and have a mission statement to direct them in their efforts. Having been in an administrative position for several years, I can say with certainty that it is impossible to please everyone. The school system is one administration with which I frequently come in contact as a Child and Adolescent Psychiatrist. It is inevitable that school issues will arise when working with children with psychiatric illness.

It can be very daunting for parents to try to navigate through the school administration when things are not going well for their child. Often the school can find parents when a student is disrupting the class or the lunchroom, but it becomes more difficult when parents need to find a way to get the school to accommodate their child's needs. Schools are limited in their resources, and thus parents need to be able to work with school personnel to maximize all supports for a child in need.

Expectations are High

Children are expected to attend and participate in school regardless of most circumstances, including many illnesses. School is where children need to perform, where their success is measured, where they compete. It is where parents expect them to illustrate their potential in life, to prove what they can do, what they can become. That is a tall order, especially if a child is struggling with, well, with just about anything! Imagine how difficult it is to perform at your best when tired, let alone if you have a learning disability, Anxiety, Depression, or Autism. It can be pretty tough. Adults have more autonomy to call in sick to work, ask for a transfer of departments, even decide to quit their job entirely and look for another, or not! Children, however, are expected, and rightly so, to stay the course, to persevere, and do what it takes to succeed. For children facing challenges, this is more difficult, and it is these children who need more parental and school support.

Investigate, Investigate

When a child is not succeeding in school, parents need to find out why. There are many reasons for school difficulties: learning difficulties, cognitive difficulties [ie.IQ], emotional issues, or very basic issues such as hearing and vision problems. Parents/guardians and the school firstly need to know what the true capability of a child is in order to be realistic about expectations and to provide the appropriate supports.

The first step is for parents to identify if their child is struggling in some way and to start to look into the possible reasons why. Usually this starts with a meeting with the teacher to state your concern and seek his/her opinion. Look for ways for you and the teacher to address the issue. It may be simple - maybe a seat change from another student who is distracting your child; maybe your child cannot see the board properly, etc. If you think the issue is beyond the scope of you and the classroom teacher, next try bringing in the guidance counselor. It is best for both parents, if

Chapter Nine • If I Were Principal for a Day!!

possible, to attend in order to show your unified concern to the guidance counselor and the teacher. The school may need to do an educational assessment to investigate for attentional, learning, and cognitive issues. Perhaps the guidance counselor can meet with your child individually to try to see if there are any emotional issues of concern. If this is the case, then your child should see the family physician for further investigation. Do not stop looking for answers until you are satisfied that you have found a solution.

Supports

Once a problem is identified, you will need to ensure time and time again that the appropriate supports are put in place for your child within the school setting. No one knows your child and what they need to succeed better than you. As parents, you need to educate yourself about the school system, the levels of curriculum, the support systems, all available avenues of intervention, and how to get them. School Districts will vary in what they can provide, but you need to know the exhaustive list of supports which they do have. By working collaboratively with schools, success is often achieved. Being overly defensive or demanding in any interpersonal encounter will not get as far as informed, respectful communication.

Most schools want children to succeed. Some teachers, guidance counselors, and principals are better than others, but it has been my experience that at least someone in the system is genuinely concerned about the student in question. If you are feeling that the school is not hearing you and not providing what your child needs, ask to speak with administration at the next level, like the school board level. Educational Psychologists can be very helpful and add great support to the team. Be open-minded when learning about the school's observations of your child, their objective findings, and their opinions. Be open and determined to satisfy your questions and worries. Your child is dependent on you to seek the correct supports and solutions to their challenges.

Advocate with Energy

Advocating for your child can be exhausting and intimidating even to the most seasoned of parents. Many of my patients state that they feel very insecure in the school administrative setting. Many feel they are made to feel insecure and that they are met with condescending attitudes. This can discourage many parents from approaching the teacher or principal with a concern. Many parents are reluctant to address an issue with a teacher for fear of further recrimination or hardship towards their child. But by giving into this train of thought, parents are allowing inappropriate behaviour to continue, similar to giving in to the bully. Important issues of concern can be addressed professionally and calmly. State your concern, if you have it, about repercussions on your child. State plainly and respectfully if you feel your concerns are being marginalized or not being taken seriously. If you feel someone is being condescending to you, say so. By using clear, concise, respectful communication, you can get your message across, usually come to a better place of understanding, and create a better learning environment for your child.

Get Informed

Many 'Behaviours' can be misunderstood, especially those symptoms of Attention Deficit Hyperactivity Disorder (ADHD) and Anxiety. ADHD children may find it difficult to sit still for long, so they may need to take frequent breaks and move around. They may impulsively blurt out things like answers to questions, but more likely silly comments, words of frustration, many of which are ill-timed. An impulsive child may not be thinking anything much different from his non-ADHD classmate, but he just can't keep it to himself or lets his comment come out at just the wrong time! Children with anxiety can be very oppositional when asked to stand up in class and read aloud or answer a math question. They may be refusing to come into the classroom, clinging onto Mom, not out of obstinance, but sheer fear. The ADHD child may need an extra gym class or free visits to the guidance office for a brief walk to get rid of some of their energy. Balancing exercises are known to help working memory, which is needed for math. The anxious child needs support around his or her anxieties, and the parent also needs tremendous support to leave an anxious child behind crying! Information and knowledge are power for parent, child, and school. If your child has a medical condition which requires specific knowledge sharing and specific supports, it's your job to find out all you can about it and ensure the school also gets this information.

How To

A suggested script to look for help at school could sound like this: "Thanks for meeting with us! We are very concerned regarding our child's difficulty with....We really appreciate your support, and value your observations. As parents we would like you to..."

Your child may be having peer issues and needs help with social skills, or there is a learning challenge/disability that requires extra support. They may need help with their extra energy level or need breaks from the classroom. Get to know what your child needs and what the school may be able to provide.

Using the email system can really help with communication as parents can check homework web sites, etc. Make sure you use every service available to you to improve the relationship between you, your child, and the school. Be persistent but cooperative with the school. School is an important place for your child to know how to navigate through. School is an important place not only for academics, but also for social development. Your lead with how you negotiate with the school is being closely watched by your child.

A suggested script for a parent feeling frustrated with a school representative could be: "Thanks so much for meeting with us and for all your support so far with our child. We have serious concerns about our child's issues with attention. We as parents are doing all we can, yet when I come into the school to pick up my child and speak with you [the teacher] about his day, I feel I am met with a critical attitude. It is really important to me that we work together to maximize supports for my child and find the appropriate solutions. Your input is really important to me, and I value your observations and support."

It is my experience that parents often feel that a teacher is over-reporting issues about their child, when actually the teacher is usually just trying to be complete in their observations. The teacher doesn't know where you as parents may be in the recognition/understanding of the issue, what you require as far as information in order to address the issue, and where you are in the whole process. So be respectful and explicit in what you need from them as teachers and school administration. Having them involved in the process as much as possible will go a long way in keeping communication and expectations clear.

The school system is far from perfect, but the trick is to know what your child needs and try to fill in the blanks. It is difficult to

Chapter Nine • If I Were Principal for a Day!!

replace the role of the school, especially in the area of socialization of children, but we are dealing with an imperfect system that needs tweaking for our individual children. So find out what your child really needs from the school and do what you can to help them provide it. Then see what's missing and try to fill in the blanks! For example, you may find that the solution is simple or may need a little finesse. Maybe communication needs to be clearer. Email can be very effective in this area. The disorganized student may need to email assignments to avoid losing them. Maybe as the parent, you need to be more on top of assignment and test dates to help your child stay more organized. The new junior high student may feel intimidated by the teacher and need to meet with him or her, with you, to clarify issues. Maybe a learning disability in reading is making math impossible. Seek and you shall find! The answers and solutions are there somewhere. And even small changes can make enormous differences for your child. Occasionally a whole new direction needs considering, like home schooling or a new school. Remember that there is always more than one way to success. Once success begins, it continues to grow. Once a child starts to feel successful, it encourages him to continue, and continue, and continue.

If Teen Protests

Not all teens are comfortable with parents going to the 'Office' on their behalf. If your teen is protesting loudly, but has a school issue, negotiate with your teen about how they could address the issue. Make a plan with them, give them advice, and follow the issue closely. If you are not satisfied that a resolution has been found and the issue remains, then think seriously about stepping in. It is hard enough for parents to negotiate the 'system', let alone teens. The 'savvy" parent needs to keep in mind that teens are still children after all.

The Other Stuff...

Children not only are expected to perform at school, but also at ballet, piano, hockey, and on and on. The expectations are likely much greater on our children than they ever were on us at their age. And not only are today's children involved in other activities outside of school, they are often involved in a lot of them, and a lot of these activities are very competitive. Parents, coaches, and instructors alike can have very high expectations on a child, and the child and adult may be on very different pages. There is a fine line in these activities where a parent should and should not step.

I myself entered what I call the 'twilight zone of minor hockey' last year. As a novice 'hockey' parent, I was new to the world of referees, coaches, hockey parents (by the way, I have met some of my dearest friends here) and elusive schedules. Many parents will say this, that in advocating for your child in this activity, as in many others, you risk your child getting on the 'naughty list' (it's close to Christmas). Children are often more concerned about the extracurricular events than school, and can get very upset with perceived failures, or under achievements. They want to succeed, and they want everyone they know to come watch them! So this is big stuff for them. So as a parent or guardian, how do you navigate through the particular system, which likely doesn't have much of a process? Well asking other parents can be helpful; anyone who has been involved in the activity has probably run into the same issues and may have some knowledge to share with you. Each activity has its own culture, so here's your chance to be multi-cultural! Do your research, check out the association, club or program, and see what process does exist. If you feel you need to speak to someone about a concern, plan out what you want to say (see communication chapter). Maybe write out your questions or concerns. Make notes, or bring a buddy with you. Be clear and respectful. Your concerns may be easily and satisfactorily addressed. If you feel you need to go further, do so. Let the person with whom you are speaking know that this activity is really important for you and your child, and you are interested in finding a solution for your concerns. A calm, sincere approach will be helpful.

Points to Remember

School systems are not perfect, but as parents advocating for your child, you can help maximize their efforts.

Most schools want to help. Find someone in the system that you connect with as a direct link!

Be the detective; find the source of the problem, brainstorm about solutions with someone who could help, and advocate for help. You know what works for your child more than anyone. Be assertive in making suggestions you know could help your child learn better, or feel more comfortable in the classroom and school.

Be persistent, don't give up. Solutions are there. The school has many people to serve; your child needs you to be persistent to make sure they get what they need. Be the squeaky wheel!

Don't let a 'Label' form of thinking sway you from advocating for your child's needs. A child's disruptive or demanding behaviour and difficulties form unfavorable opinions, not solutions and progress! Be open-minded and supportive.

Don't let the unknown system scare you off from advocating for your child, just get informed. Ask other parents, do some research, and step cautiously. A solution is there-you just may need a more circuitous route to find it.

"Reading the road signs helps us make the right turn."
Fr.JJM

Chapter Ten

ADHD: The Child Who Just Can't PAY ATTENTION!

I see a lot of children with attention deficit hyperactivity disorder or ADHD in my practice. It is a very rewarding medical condition to treat because children and their families benefit tremendously when they receive the correct diagnosis and treatments. I won't get into all the details of this medical condition, but I'll provide an overview of its symptoms and treatments. I feel it is important to mention this condition because when ADHD is left undiagnosed and the child suffering from this condition is deprived from appropriate diagnosis and intervention, it can be tremendously stressful on the child and family. Children with this disorder also have a high incidence of other problems, such as learning difficulties, or may develop other behavioural conditions like oppositional defiant disorder. Early detection for all medical conditions is better for the patient, and ADHD is no different.

Appropriate intervention can save a child and their family an enormous amount of grief. The resources for child and adolescent mental health issues do not meet the demand, and so children with these issues can be missed. Schools may not be adequately informed, parents are often not led in the right direction, and stigma interferes considerably with some parents' approach to this issue. Become educated, inform yourself, and don't allow the destructiveness of stigma and ignorance in our society to rob your child and you of the right to appropriate medical attention!

ADHD is, unfortunately, relatively common. Depending on the study you read, the percentage of children with this disorder ranges significantly, though an average estimate is about five percent. Every child with ADHD looks a little different, as all children are unique. Some may have more inattention, others may have more energized activity, and some may have more impulsiveness. The hyperactivity part confuses people, as the hyperactivity, like all the symptoms, can vary considerably between patients. Hyperactivity can mean the child has great difficulty sitting still or is often running around and seldom in one place for long. Hyperactivity can be fidgetiness, tapping the pencil at their desk, or squirming around a lot when sitting. Some students with hyperactivity often need to get up in class and walk around, go to the bathroom, sharpen a pencil, or whatever!

These are not the type of behaviours that teachers like to see or can tolerate well without explanation. Lots of children are more hyperactive when younger, but settle down a bit as they mature with age. All children can be hyperactive at times; it is a matter of intensity and consistency. Like many medical symptoms, there is a range from normal to the abnormal, and a point at which the symptoms consistently interfere with the patient. Take a headache, for example. Most of us get headaches, but they usually are short-lived and only occur occasionally. Easily treated, we can often push through them and carry on with normal activity. Well, it's the same with hyperactivity. If it is occasional, responds to limit setting, and does not interfere with usual activities, it's normal. If it is persistent, difficult to control, and interfering with normal

Chapter Ten • ADHD: The Child Who Just Can't PAY ATTENTION!

activities and development, it needs some attention!

Unfocused...

The other hallmark symptoms of ADHD are inattention, distractibility and impulsiveness. Again, there are spectrums of normal to abnormal for all these symptoms as well. Let's take inattention and distractibility first. Remember that children want to succeed, do well with activities, appear successful to peers, and fit in. They want to please parents and teachers and they want to get on with things like homework so they can go out and play! So when this is not happening, there is a reason for this. Most children, if they do not suffer from learning difficulties, should be able to get homework done fairly quickly and independently. Remember that the material has been reviewed in class; they are expected to work fairly independently in class, with usually one teacher to many students. They don't get much one-on-one in class, so they do learn to work on their own fairly quickly. Homework should usually take under half an hour. Check with the teacher and other parents as to how long they feel it should take to do homework.

If your child is consistently trying to avoid homework by looking for a drink, a pencil, or wanting to do something in the middle of a math sheet, like call his buddy about soccer, go to the bathroom three times, pick at his little brother, or whatever else pops up in his mind, he is probably having sincere difficulty maintaining his attention and finds it equally difficult to shut out distractions when necessary. Homework is when we see these symptoms - when a child is required to do something that, while necessary, is not high on the fun list. We all do activities with much more enthusiasm and with little prompting when we are motivated and find them fun and entertaining. Children with ADHD experience this same phenomenon, but to greater degrees. Homework is a great challenge since their attention span is limited and they are not strongly motivated (let's face it, homework equates to paying bills for us - not exciting, but has to be done!). Children with an appropriate attention span and normal levels of distractibility will get through it much quicker and more easily, and move on to the fun stuff. They can look forward to the fun stuff and plan around that much more easily than a child with ADHD.

Acting before Thinking

Impulsiveness is a symptom that can cause difficulties in a number of areas for a child. Impulsiveness is when you say or do something quickly, without thinking about it too much. Children who are impulsive may spontaneously answer out of turn in class, interrupt conversations, or act out aggressively. These children are usually remorseful about their behaviour - they don't want to be irritating to their friends or family, but their impulsive behaviour can be very frustrating to others and can lead to social rejection. Other children can find another child's impulsiveness aggravating and slowly stop wanting to be around him or her. It is taxing for the parent of a child who is impulsive, so imagine how others who don't really love your child can tire of this behaviour.

Exclusion

Social isolation doesn't happen to all impulsive children, but if they are also hyperactive and inattentive, it can be overwhelming to others. Children want to belong, and it is very hurtful to them if their peers don't include them. Social isolation, if it occurs, I feel is one of the most significant fallouts with ADHD. Impulsiveness can also be dangerous and cause isolation. Children can run into the street, since they don't think about the risk of a situation,

Chapter Ten • ADHD: The Child Who Just Can't PAY ATTENTION!

and can get themselves into sticky situations. Adolescents with ADHD who drive have more accidents because of inattention and increased risk taking. These adolescents are also at risk of making more impulsive decisions about a lot of things they are exposed to like drinking, drugs, and sex. Adolescence is challenging enough - being impulsive and inattentive can really shake things up!

Organization is Key to Success

Executive Functioning is a huge issue for children with ADHD. Our executive functioning is what helps us plan things, organize, anticipate, and trouble shoot. People with ADHD don't do this well! Students with poor organizational skills will often forget homework, assignments, and if remembered and completed, will then lose them (sometimes even from home to the locker). A teen may swear she passed in the assignment, think she did, and then find it at the bottom of the book bag! Parents will often think their child is not telling the truth to avoid reprimand, but the fact is that their teen (with ADHD) really did believe the assignment was passed in. When organization is an issue, I suggest to teens and parents that they email or mail in a copy of the assignment to the teacher whenever possible.

As parents you need to be even more prepared, organized, and creative when you have a child/teen with ADHD. You need to understand the natural difficulties of the condition, be realistic about what your child can undertake, be responsible for, and be independent about. If your expectations are realistic, whether your child has a full-blown diagnosis or simply weaknesses in these important areas, you can rise to the organizational needs of your child. Good role modeling, example setting, and teaching in this area will lead to a smoother day for both you and your child. They will learn from your organizational example. You are the most valuable teacher to your child. You have the most access to them, the most insight and the most influence. Make the most of it! If you find that you yourself are no better organized than they are, maybe you should take a closer look at your own needs. The apple doesn't usually fall too far from the tree - ADHD does run in families! So if you cannot give much organizational guidance, find someone who can help both of you.

The Fall-out

Children with ADHD are at a much greater risk of many things. Their difficulties with focus can lead to poor academic achievement, poor social connections, and strained relationships both at school and at home. Self esteem can become an issue, and so "popularity" may be sought in less appropriate ways. When children end up on the social periphery, trouble can soon follow! Being on the social fringe and somewhat impulsive can then lead to poor lifestyle choices. Drugs are like smarties, alcohol is like milk, and sex is more and more common in younger and younger youth. Children and teens today have a lot to deal with, which is made even more difficult if they are somewhat rejected by peers, low on self esteem, and quick to jump in. Our children really need lots of good parental influence and presence, especially when experiencing their own chaos. And believe me, ADHD can be chaos! Children with ADHD also have a much greater chance of having a learning disability or other behavioural disorder like oppositional defiant disorder (when there is a basic disregard for authority) or conduct disorder (a basic disregard for the rights of others) or a mood or anxiety disorder.

Chapter Ten • ADHD: The Child Who Just Can't PAY ATTENTION!

How to Explore Further

The diagnosis of ADHD is a clinical diagnosis, based primarily on the child's history, the description of his or her difficulties and how they interfere with his or her progress. Often parents ask me to test for ADHD, which is really not how it is done! While some questionnaires are used, especially ones for teachers to fill out, review of report cards and current collateral history from school, daycare, and activity leaders is also helpful. The diagnosis is based primarily on history provided by the child and family and symptom description from the child.

Treatments range from behavioural interventions to medications. Education about the condition is essential for the family, child, and usually school if the family wants them to be involved. Understanding symptoms is the first step in learning how to accept and manage them. Expectations need to be realistic and support appropriate. The right treatment can change a child's life for the better!

While the choice to use medication is a big one for both the physician and family, research has shown that medication is usually necessary to improve symptoms of inattention, impulsivity, and hyperactivity. Many children respond well to medication and the improvements can be startling! ADHD is a neurodevelopment medical condition involving neurotransmitters and certain parts of the brain involved with attention and impulsivity. It stands to reason that a medical condition requires medication for symptom control. This, however, can be very challenging for parents to wrap their heads around. Starting your child on any medication is difficult, and since the symptoms of ADHD start from a spectrum of normal, many parents feel that the child can improve functioning with the right motivation. If that was the case, most children with ADHD would not make it to our (physicians') offices, and that is definitely not the case!! Also a high percentage of children continue to have symptoms into late adolescence and adulthood. So if their parents couldn't accept the need for treatment, they will often seek it as older teens or adults to achieve a better quality of life.

Be Open

Be open-minded and accepting. A correct diagnosis does not label a child; it actually frees them of considerable dysfunction and turmoil when appropriately treated. You wouldn't ignore symptoms of diabetes, asthma, or juvenile arthritis, so don't downplay behavioural symptoms that are labeling and disabling your child! ADHD is a real medical condition of the brain, but the signs are behavioural, which can trick parents and society into thinking kids can control it if they really wanted to. What was it that guy Lennon said, "Give Peace a Chance"??!! So be open about this issue, be open to your own child, or your child's friend who may have this diagnosis. Don't be judgmental. Be supportive.

Chapter Ten • ADHD: The Child Who Just Can't PAY ATTENTION!

Points to Remember:

Attention deficit hyperactivity disorder looks a little different for every child who has it! The main symptoms are persistent problems with a short attention span, distractibility, impulsivity, and increased activity level. There are usually problems with organization, planning, and emotional instability. If a child is quiet and not paying attention, they may not reach the teacher's radar! Not all children with ADHD are causing trouble for others, just themselves!

ADHD is a medical condition that requires appropriate diagnosis and treatment. There is no specific "test" for ADHD - it is a clinical diagnosis, made through history and symptom assessment.

Symptoms of ADHD can be disabling in a number of areas, such as academics, social functioning, and family relationships.

This is a real medical condition that may significantly improve with treatment, greatly benefiting both child and family.

Children with ADHD have a greater chance of other behavioural conditions, learning disabilities, and other psychiatric conditions.

"To bring love into life we have to begin at home."
Mother Theresa of Calcutta

Chapter Eleven

Anxiety and Depression: Our Worried and Sad Children

Anxiety and depression are often thought of as adult conditions, but unfortunately many children and adolescents are afflicted with both. I will give a brief overview of these medical conditions, both of which can be devastating to child and family.

Anxiety and worry are a spectrum of feelings. Everyone needs a little anxiety, to help get the test studied for, the job interview prepared, the wedding planned. However, anyone who has experienced panic, and couldn't get the test completed, the interview attended, or the marriage proposal out, knows that too much anxiety is rather crippling. Anyone with a child who is terrified to attend school, to allow their parents to go out at night, or attend the soccer league game they signed up for, knows their child is not faking it. Anxiety in children and adolescents is real, and it is terrifying. Often parents will describe their child as very shy, and they begin to accept that their child just cannot or does not do certain things. But these 'certain things' are usually age appropriate social interactions that are healthy and often necessary for normal development. Excessive shyness is often mistaken for a child's 'personality', but if this 'shyness' is preventing that child

Chapter Eleven • Anxiety and Depression: Our Worried and Sad Children

from participating in activities that they should be enjoying or at least not find excruciatingly difficult, there could be an anxiety disorder happening.

Anxiety disorders can occur in over 10% of school-age children. That is a lot of kids. If you have not suffered from true anxiety, imagine how you may have felt at your most anxious moment, multiply that by 100, and you get a glimpse of what it's like to have a true anxiety disorder. A child with an anxiety disorder has to overcome tremendous challenges just in order to try to experience the routine events of the normal day. There are a number of anxiety disorders of childhood, such as separation anxiety, generalized anxiety, obsessive compulsive disorder, and social anxiety. Each anxiety disorder is a medical condition with its own specific criteria or symptoms. I'll describe each one briefly and how they may affect a child. This summary and description of anxiety disorders is not meant to replace a physician's full assessment. If you have concerns about your child, you should have him or her assessed by a physician.

Separation

Separation anxiety is when a child feels intense anxiety when separated from his or her parents. The separation can be under a number of different circumstances. For example, it may be when the child has to go to school, or when either a parent or both parents go out of the house. There are many degrees of intensity for this condition; some children feel the anxiety worst on Sunday evenings when they are getting ready to start the school week again. Often by Thursday or Friday, the anxiety is less intense. Separation anxiety can start at the beginning of school in kindergarten or may first become a major issue at the change of school from elementary school to junior high, or at the beginning of high school. Some children will start with somatic complaints like headaches or stomach aches. The physical symptoms may be extremely convincing, and many children end up getting a number of investigations done to rule out a physical medical condition that may be causing the physical symptom and school refusal. Some children have intense fear if their parent or parents go out at night. They may be very clingy, and some parents find themselves unable to leave the house without their child. Some children will be fine with school but cannot participate in extracurricular activities. They may be enthusiastic about it, sign up, but then just cannot go. Parents can get confused and very frustrated! The child often ends up in the Psychiatrist's office out of desperation for an explanation of the child's symptoms and to address the intense family distress. Once a physical cause is ruled out, often the history will reveal a pattern of anxiety in milder forms, which has escalated to its current, disabling form. There are great treatments for this, including a behavioural approach, as well as medications which can be very effective. Treating this very disruptive and agonizing anxiety condition can restore a child's life and also allow the family to get back to a rewarding, loving routine with their child, without the intense pressure of dealing with this very interfering medical condition.

Social Fear

Social anxiety is also a very disruptive anxiety condition. In this disorder, children and adolescents have an intense fear of embarrassment and will avoid being the centre of attention at all cost. These children can also have difficulty attending school, and, when they do, they do not want to interact in the classroom by answering questions or asking questions if they need clarification. They shy away from people of authority and basically try to blend

Chapter Eleven • Anxiety and Depression: Our Worried and Sad Children

in with the wallpaper. Peer interactions can be more anxiety-provoking than interacting with adults, as the peer group is considered more 'important' to them. Social anxiety can keep children and adolescents isolated socially and make academic progress difficult. Many teens will get through high school, but may not even consider post-secondary schooling due to their high levels of anxiety. Meeting new people and dating can be very challenging. Many people with social anxiety may self medicate with alcohol to help take the edge off the anxiety in social situations. It unfortunately does help with the anxiety temporarily, but can lead to a whole set of other problems. Again, parents may make the assumption that their child is just very shy, but when anxiety interferes with school attendance and the ability to make social connections expected for their age group, then shyness has crossed the threshold to anxiety.

Generalized Fear

Generalized anxiety is characterized by an intense anxiety that is more often present than not and can occur in any setting. These children have overwhelming anticipatory anxiety, worrying about what is to come and spending a lot of their time in that zone. Rumination about what was said, what they did or didn't do, generalized fears, often about nothing they can fully explain - they just feel fearful. It is difficult to carry on as a 10 year-old or a 16 year-old when you are always worried. There are varying degrees of anxiety levels, but anyone with an anxiety disorder is having way too much anxiety. I see some children who panic about performance and may have exam anxiety. Some children are fearful of specific issues and may seem isolated in nature, but it is usually just that the generalized anxiety is manifesting in certain circumstances, like not being able to go to a sporting event or a party or feeling fretful in general. There can be significant overlap between these three anxiety disorders, but what is most important is that a child with anxiety is identified and helped.

Over and Over Again

Obsessive compulsive disorder (or OCD) is an anxiety disorder where a person experiences unwanted, obtrusive, and repetitive thoughts and/or repetitive actions they cannot resist. Often the person with OCD has a fear of something which the compulsive action will somehow fix. For example, a fear of contamination may lead to hand washing. OCD is often dubbed the 'hidden disorder' as many children and adolescents don't want to talk about it because they are embarrassed about the symptoms. Sometimes the repetitive, intrusive thoughts are bizarre and not something the child or adolescent would ever voluntarily think. Sometimes the thoughts may be of an aggressive or sexual nature and are very distressing to the person. By definition of the disorder, these thoughts are recurrent, ridiculous, and are resisted, but not successfully. The repetitive actions are also seen by the child as unusual and not appropriate, but resisting them initially creates a significant increase in anxiety. Children can become very clever in hiding their compulsive actions, and adolescents in keeping their distressing thoughts to themselves. It is very important when assessing someone in psychiatry that specific questions about OCD are asked directly. I have had patients with OCD at varying intensities, some almost immobilized with the obsessions and compulsions, while others show only minor symptoms.

Often children hide their symptoms for years from their parents. They have been counting things for years, dealing with issues of symmetry, like brushing their hair the same number of times on each side, erasing homework over and over due to imperfection,

Chapter Eleven • Anxiety and Depression: Our Worried and Sad Children

and tidying up the front closet of shoes to reinstate order. Often the parents themselves may have had some minor obsessions so they don't really see anything unusual or may just think the child will outgrow it, as they may have. Teens will be more reluctant than younger children to discuss any bizarre thoughts for fear of judgment. OCD can be very debilitating and frustrating, to child and parent as well. Obsessive slowness, due to checking and rechecking, recurrent rituals in the bathroom can make everyone in the household late for their day. Some children have to check everything that happened in the day with their parent(s). These behaviours can be very distressing and frustrating, interfering terribly with a child's health and progress.

Depression

Depression can wear many faces and can be very confusing to parents and children alike. Like anxiety, depression is a real medical condition. It can happen to anyone, male and female, and of any circumstance. A family history of depression increases a child's chances of getting depression. It is uncommon to see depression in pre-pubertal children, but it can happen, especially with a strong family history of depression or with excessive stress, like the death of a parent. Anxiety and depression often go together; it can sometimes be hard to say what may have started first, but that's okay, since both medical conditions are treated by the same medicine, and talk therapy (psychotherapy) should also happen for both.

Depression in children and adolescents can present with primarily an irritable mood, as opposed to an outright depressed mood. A child or teen can be very snappy, difficult to talk to, and isolative from family. And what's so new about that, you may think, in a lot of teens! But a depressed child will have persistent symptoms like irritability, poor sleep, change in appetite, loss of interest in regular activities, poor concentration, feelings of worthlessness and hopelessness, anger, and sometimes thoughts of wanting to die. These children will say it is difficult for them to feel happy and have fun. Every teen or child will have a different combination of symptoms, but the biggest change is usually a significant, persistent feeling of irritability. There is usually a change from previous temperament and mood, and a change in performance in many ways, especially school. A child who has a quiet or shy temperament may be more difficult to see a change in, and sometimes the onset is insidious and sometimes sudden. A child with any other medical condition can also be a little more difficult to identify as having a depressive illness. Substance abuse can also be a complicating factor.

Lots of children and teens will have stress and some difficult periods in their lives. Depressive illness is a persistent change in mood and, usually, functioning. Be aware of the warning signs and, if you see them or just suspect something is not right, look a little further, get an appropriate medical assessment and advice. Be very involved. Parents and families are an instrumental part of the solution.

The Good News

Many people are amazed to learn that children and adolescents can suffer such distressing symptoms and medical disorders. Fortunately, there are good treatments and most children can make significant progress. Of course, a proper assessment by a trained mental health professional is necessary if there is suspicion of an anxiety disorder. As a parent, being informed is helpful; following your instinct when you have a concern about your child is imperative. Stigma against mental illness hurts children

Chapter Eleven • Anxiety and Depression: Our Worried and Sad Children

especially, as they depend on others to advocate for them. Anxiety disorders, like many other medical conditions, run in families, so if there is a family history of anxiety and a child has some concerning issues, a closer look is important. Successful treatment of any medical condition is possible only once the condition is identified. Some parents tell me initially that they don't want their child labeled. That wouldn't be the case if they were seeing an oncologist or dermatologist. They would want a correct diagnosis or 'label' in order to get the correct treatment. Insulin would not be held back for a child with insulin dependent diabetes mellitus. A pancreas cannot be talked into working correctly, just as a child with an anxiety disorder cannot be expected to 'shake it off' without the appropriate medical management. Often this consists of behavioural management and possibly medication. Details of treatment are beyond the scope of this book, but they can be very effective and can restore a child to their state of health and a family to a state of peace. Open-mindedness and appropriate assessment, if necessary, can make a beautiful child able to have a beautiful life.

Parents have an important role to play in helping their children cope with their anxiety. A child with anxiety will often jump to catastrophic thinking about an issue or event. For example, a child or adolescent who is worried about failing a test may start by thinking, "I can't do this, I am going to fail, actually I am going to fail the whole course, then I'll fail the year, and then I will likely not pass school at all and never get anywhere in life…I'll lose my friends, my family will reject me…" and so on. The domino effect of negative thinking is set into motion. Thoughts lead to feelings, so this type of negative thinking can cause some very negative feelings, anxiety, and depressive feelings as well. It is important to interrupt the negative thinking by challenging the negative thoughts with more realistic thinking. For example, you can point out in the above example that "you prepared for the test and that is the most important step. You usually do fine in tests, it is only a test and not the final grade, this is only one course and you are doing fine in the other courses, and even if you happen to do 'not so great' on the test, we will still love and support you".

Helping a child see things more realistically without the veil of anxiety and negativity will help him or her feel better about it. Being supportive is important, but it is also very important not to facilitate the anxiety. This can happen if the parent is too sympathetic, if they seem to be validating the negative thinking. For example, if a child states something like, "I just can't do it, and I never will be able to do it, even though I really want to", and the parent says something like, "I know how you feel," and then gets pulled into the negativity, they will likely increase the anxiety by giving the message that the child should feel this way. It's like feeling panic when a child falls and scrapes their knee. If the parent panics and overreacts, the child is much more likely to cry and panic. If the parent is calm, reassuring and directive to recovery, the child usually bounces back quickly. So must the parent act in a directive, positive, and calm manner when a child feels anxiety or fear. Being supportive and directive, by saying something like, "I know it must feel really scary right now, but why don't we try looking at it a little differently…" and point out the more realistic, positive angle on the situation. This approach will be much more effective in helping the child feel calm and in control. As a parent, you need to be in touch with what makes you feel anxious and scared, as your children will pick up on this very fast.

Just because you are afraid of dogs, heights, or being alone, you don't want your kids to learn this. It is important to be aware of your fears, to guard against passing them on, and to help your child face their fears. A positive, realistic approach to accurate thoughts

Chapter Eleven • Anxiety and Depression: Our Worried and Sad Children

about a fear can be very powerful in turning around a scary situation. Remember that role modeling is important; children will learn what they live, and your children are watching your every move, word, and action. So get in touch with your fears, try to deal with them, or at least learn how to approach them with a positive, realistic thinking pattern. This will illustrate to your children just how it is done! Every child will have some fears, even if they are not true anxieties, and need help in learning how to deal with them. Parents are instrumental in role modeling coping strategies to their children. Educate yourself about how best to do this if you feel you are struggling in a particular area. Being informed, learning how to do it right, helps tremendously. If you are unsure of something, ask someone who can help, think about taking a parenting course, see a psychologist who works with children to seek advice. There are many ways to improve your skills in this area. Motivation is key; the rest usually falls into place!

Points to Remember

Some anxiety is needed; excessive anxiety is debilitating!

Lots of kids get anxiety disorders, which are real medical conditions, with real medical treatments!

Be aware of your own anxieties and how they may be influencing your child.

And remember, the apple doesn't usually fall far from the tree. If you had an anxiety or depressive disorder as a child and outgrew it without medical intervention, it doesn't mean your child can do it without intervention. The earlier in life that a child manifests a mental medical condition, the more strength it usually has. So your child may have a 'bigger dose' of it than you did.

If you suspect something may be wrong, trust yourself and get help for your child. There is help to be had and peace to be felt. Don't short change your child from appropriate medical help.

Learn how to help. You are very important in your child's recovery from an anxiety disorder or depression.

It is very rewarding as a child psychiatrist to treat children with anxiety conditions. They mostly do very well with appropriate intervention, and their lives and their families' lives improve dramatically! So, chin up!!

> *"We bank our credit when we pay attention to our loved ones!"*
> *Fr. JJM*

Chapter Twelve

Humour: Laughter Really Is the Best Medicine

I am beginning to write this chapter just at the start of the flu season, H1N1 flu season, so it is challenging for most of us to feel light, especially if you have children and elderly parents! But maybe it will help put things into perspective, hopefully without tragedy. Unfortunately, it often takes some sort of dramatic event or tragedy to shake us into change. It is very progressive for most of us to make changes because we see it as important, and not because a dramatic incident has occurred. So let's try to insert levity and laughter just for the fun of it!

Humor is actually classified as a mature coping mechanism in the world of psychiatry. How many wakes have you attended where the family is cracking jokes about their deceased loved one or just joking around in general? It happens a lot in Newfoundland, and I think it reflects the need to lighten up a very sad, intense event that, without perspective, would be paralyzingly tragic. The humor helps us cope, to stay standing. So stand tall, and laugh and laugh!

Lighten Up

I often find myself talking to my patients and their families about not taking themselves too seriously and the importance of having fun together. This is extremely important to maintaining close connections within your family, especially when things get tough. Most of us take life very, very seriously. We get dug into the day-to-day trenches, and details can side track us away from the main event. In order to help our children learn to put things into perspective, we as parents first need to pay attention to this issue. By getting uptight about the exactness of an issue, the precise execution of a task, or the absolute result, we waste a lot of time and create angst and tension for everyone involved. To take ourselves a little lighter, to be able to laugh at ourselves and be forgiving of our shortcomings, is a very powerful example to our child of strong self esteem, self acceptance, and personal insight - all instrumental qualities to a healthy mind.

As you drop your cell phone into the toilet, forget to register on time for your spinning class, or fall off your newest health routine, your child is watching and learning from your reaction pattern. If you rant and rave, blame yourself harshly, call yourself stupid or weak, boy, what a powerful message you are sending! It screams lack of tolerance for self, mistakes, and lack of perfection. I wonder how the witness of this would feel about going to you about forgetting a test date, breaking or losing their cell phone, or looking for advice about how to get back on their fitness routine – a little scared of judgment, I would guess! However, if the events of minor disaster were seen as an opportunity for a little laugh, recognition of a better plan, acknowledgement and acceptance of personal areas of need, and an opportunity to think of new ways around the challenge, this would send a much healthier, useful

Chapter Twelve • Humour: Laughter Really Is the Best Medicine

message. It would illustrate personal tolerance, perspective, and the ability to reorganize and plan another, maybe more helpful, approach to an issue.

Looking at what is funny about a situation and adjusting what is necessary, learning a lesson even, is not being dismissive. It is approaching a non-life threatening situation with reason, insight, and levity. We can't laugh through all our mishaps and misfortunes, but the lighter side is helpful, easier to recover from, and helps us see more options. Being open about the situation allows more discussion, and usually this helps bring in more options and a better resolution. So the next time you wash your kid's cell phone in the 40-minute wash cycle, take out the hair dryer, take 10 deep breaths, marvel at the fact that it was the first time this year your son brought his dirty clothes out of his room, and have a little chuckle at the irony of that! Then discuss with Johnny the importance of going through pockets as the clothes enter the washing machine, look at a fundraising plan should the phone not revive, and then lend him yours for his current peace of mind! Maybe it will be a stepping stone to his first bonafide job!! Something good is never far away!

So now that you are giggling your way through your tax return, you can approach your children's dilemmas, disasters, and perceived failures with more ease and light-heartedness. This is not to be confused with being dismissive about what is important to your child, but to learn to sift through what really is important, what is trivial and what is fixable, and to teach this to your child. Children see their world through their cognitive perspective. When your nine year-old says his three day-old underwear is not dirty, he doesn't need a bath, and that he'll be fine staying up until midnight watching X-Men, he is saying the truth - the truth as he sees it! When your teen says she won't be late - "What! 1:00 am is NOT late Mom." and her room looks 'fine' - she really does see it that way. She is not trying to be argumentative; she is just expressing her point of view. Jostle her about tornado watches, close the bedroom door, and remind her that the more sleep she gets before midnight, the better her skin will be!

Make sure that you hold your ground on important issues, but keeping it light will help your child let go of the issue more easily. Firmness, without ambivalence, mingled with respectful humour, can settle a lot of sticky situations with less trauma than expected. Discipline with humour, not sarcasm, which can come across as disrespect, will teach your child to keep things in perspective. There is nothing more disrespectful than nasty sarcasm or condescending dismissiveness. So be careful to be sensitive and respectful in your humour, and it will likely be well-received. If your child perceives your lightheartedness as uncaring or condescending, apologize and explain what you were thinking. Take the opportunity to discuss the situation, and try to add a new dimension of perspective your child is not seeing.

Time to Play!

Playing with your children creates closeness and an ease of being together. Playing with your teen is not all that different from playing with your toddler. You pick something she'll likely enjoy, at a time convenient for both of you (not her Friday night with friends time or your yoga time!). We need to make special effort to spend time with our teen children, as they feel intense need to be with friends, they have many demands, and we as parents sometimes assume they don't want to be around us. But most teens I talk to want to spend more time with their parents, having fun with them, not discussing homework. So no matter what the day has brought, or what conflict may be brewing between you and yours, try to keep

Chapter Twelve • Humour: Laughter Really Is the Best Medicine

that date and go out to have fun. The break from the serious will make it easier to address the serious!

A weekend can go very fast! I feel much more satisfied when I know I have spent quality time together as a family having fun. Games, swimming, biking, cards, reading together, and mostly laughing together make the times good. Laughter is so important; it creates intense pleasure and lasting good feelings. A good laugh stands out in your mind. Children especially remember the 'FUN' and value it tremendously (see the last chapter). Don't miss out on the opportunity to laugh with your children. You will both feel good and closer as a result. Having fun together is tremendously bonding. So try to actually make opportunities for fun to happen. Sometimes it is more fun for the child than the parent, but just try to relax into the fun - the payoff is tremendous! Try it, you will definitely like it.

Being Self Aware

It can sometimes be pretty challenging to find the humor in situations, as a stressed parent with many demands, fluctuating hormones, worry about our children, and, did I mention, fluctuating hormones. But it is good for us and our kids! When angry, stay away from sharp objects and, when able, take a breath, smile, and remember that what is happening is not [usually] life or death and will likely be a topic to chuckle about in a few hours. Even what may seem disastrous can become humorous. We just need to look at it a little differently; maybe we just need some time away from it. So as we learn to use humour, we can help our children use humor appropriately. Turning strife to chuckles and making a point to actually have fun when not stressed, will bring us closer to our children and go a long way in de-stressing ourselves. Have fun; it's very important!!

Points to Remember

Having fun together as a family is very important. It helps build bonds, strengthens relationships, and relaxes people! So when the going gets tough, there is a good solid foundation. When we think of friends, we usually think of the fun we had together, not the serious conversations. The laughs are what we remember, and this fun stuff is what helps make us close.

Children and teens want to spend time with family. It may not be as easy as when they were younger, but with creativity, can be even more fun.

Most serious situations are only serious for a short time, Remember that when you're about to blow. Wait a few minutes, and you may just find the humour in it.

Not taking yourself too seriously is very useful in keeping yourself and life in perspective. Keeping yourself grounded in the knowledge that most issues are not life-threatening and that perfection is not necessary will help you and your child. By teaching them this, you will help them tremendously to keep things in perspective!

'If laughter is the best medicine,
we don't need the doctor!"
Fr.JJM

Chapter Thirteen

Stamina- Parenting a Child with Mental Illness, Now That's Stamina!!

Parenting is usually challenging enough on a good day, with an easy child. There is not a child around who is easy all the time, but a child suffering from a psychiatric medical condition is seldom easy! Whether the diagnosis is anxiety, OCD (obsessive compulsive disorder), ADHD, depression, aspergers, a learning disability, or whatever it may be, parents have their work cut out for them! Not only do these parents have to deal with very challenging issues with their children, but they are also often confronted with many uneducated, misinformed and judgmental comments from others! There are lots of experts out there with great solutions. Some people are very supportive and well meaning, but it is really hard to truly put yourself in the shoes of these parents.

The Simple is Not So Simple

Children with mental illness of any kind will find many activities of daily living challenging. And if it doesn't bother the child, it still may be driving their parents around the block! The parents who deal best with this kind of stress tend to be able to take things a bit lighter in general. They can keep things in perspective better, can laugh out loud at things that bother them, and not 'sweat the small stuff'. This is not easy to do, since we all know, there is no bigger stress than a sick child, sick in any way, let alone sick with a chronic, interfering illness.

Children with an emotional or behavioural condition do not have the same capability for flexibility and adaptability as children without these problems. Take the morning routine, for example. This is usually tough enough for any family to get through without someone yelling, grumbling, or freaking out because Mom has left the keys to her office in her father's car which is across town and she has to be to work in ten minutes! Yeah, stuff happens! So now throw in some real obstacles: the ADHD child who never gets to sleep before midnight, and is so dog tired he can never get out of bed before 10 minutes before the bus comes; or the ten year-old with OCD who needs 45 minutes in the one bathroom in the house to shower and re-shower; or the anxious child who is screaming and crying because she is too scared to get on the bus or get in the car to go to school.

These are just a few examples. One parent was telling me how she follows her 8 year-old little girl around all morning [Mom is up an hour earlier to get herself fully work ready] to get dressed, cleaned up, fed, and out the door. She laughs as she tells me what she really wants to do with the shirt she is holding for her daughter as her child sits on her bed, naked, looking off into yonder, not even acknowledging that her mother is trying to rush her along, for the past 20 minutes! These parents know the true definition of patience, perseverance, and commitment. They are amazingly restrained as their teen with OCD tells them that the more they are asked to do something, the less they want to do it!

Homework Heck

Now let's take homework. Have you ever tried to feed a six month-old baby pabulum with a 10-foot pole while standing on your head? That's almost as difficult as doing homework with a child with ADHD! Ten minutes of homework takes an hour. Assignments, if remembered to do at all, take bribes, arm twisting, and huge parental input (like doing the whole thing!) to get done at all. A child with ADHD will wiggle, squirm, get a drink, go to the bathroom, break a pencil, sharpen a pencil, get into a squabble with a sibling, tell a joke, get another drink and then spill it, all before he/she has done equation number one! It does not come naturally to these children to sit still, focus on their homework and just get it done. Now throw in a math learning disability, perhaps some anxiety and a facial tic, and you have a party!

Similar to the worst grade nine party you ever attended, where your friends ditched you, your date dumped you, your only five bucks got five fingered and Mom and Dad had told you you were grounded but you went out anyway! Welcome to 3:00-8:00 pm at these households! These children are not trying to make their parent's lives miserable - it may feel like it sometimes, but they are not. They are struggling and doing what comes naturally to them. Also, as if to further test the heroism of these parents, the laws of genetics usually don't just stop at one child with a psychiatric condition, but often bless them with two or more! Try going to hockey or yoga or getting the dishes done before 10:00 pm when little Suzy is still struggling with her spelling list. It can be very challenging!

Bring in the Troops

We can get very stuck in these situations, and so it is really important to have support and ways to decompress for both parent and child. Knowing the diagnosis, keeping things in perspective (which can become extremely challenging), and not taking the little things too seriously is key. Doing what you can and accepting both yours and your child's limitations is crucial to peace! We can get very caught up in society's ideas of what is expected, what's correct, and what our children should achieve. When you have a child with a psychiatric condition, you truly learn that each child progresses at their own unique rate and in their own way!

Be Flexible

There is no one right way to get through raising children, especially challenging children. Understanding their strengths, needs, and challenges comes second only to accepting the child you have created. The expressions, 'we are who we are' and, 'it is what it is', are very important when it comes to our children, no matter what their make up is. The range of "normal" is so vast that we are all sure to be thrown some traits in our children we wish were a little less emphasized. These traits, by the way, are usually quite similar to the parents - genetics again, but in a more unsophisticated form. So, by being accepting and respectful to the child you created, you save a lot of grief. Then, with diligence and stamina, you work on their needs with them, by using their strengths to help them overcome their challenges. Day after day after day after day! This is no easy journey! But by using patient firmness [is that a real term, it sounds good!], keeping respect going both ways, laughing together, and sometimes crying, you will arrive at your destination.

Your child truly wants to succeed - they do want to attend school and succeed in becoming an independent young adult. I see children and families progress every day in my practice. Sometimes it is slow and painful, for patient and parent alike, but progress eventually happens. With guidance and support, treatment and counseling, most children with ADHD eventually get their homework done and graduate with possible honors. Most children with Anxiety get to some sort of school, get their education, and go on to become independent young adults. Sometimes they don't always reach the goals you or they may have had, but they are still great people, with great things to offer. It may be a different picture than you imagined; goals may need to be reset, but hey, isn't that life? At the end of the day, you still have a wonderful child, with many great attributes, who is just trying to do their best. Give them and yourselves a little slack!

Give up the Guilt

Now, I am sure we are all familiar with the emotion of guilt! Oh my goodness, I didn't put my kid in piano, he'll never learn math! I should have insisted he wear his boots and now he's sick! I should have chosen that other school; she would be excelling over there! I shouldn't have yelled last night when Johnny spilled paint at 11:00 pm all over my new outfit I was going to wear to my job interview today! I wonder if I drank too much orange juice when I was pregnant. The list is endless. Having happy, well-adjusted, healthy, successful children is our expectation. Period!

When perfection doesn't happen, who you gonna call: Guilt and Company Ltd! Parenthood guilt is very powerful. Where does guilt, senseless guilt, (let's take for granted no one reading this is an actual criminal) get us? Well, sleepless nights, poor appetite, lethargy, some headaches, probably a few extra pounds we don't need, poor creativity, lack of spontaneity, few friends (who wants to be around Grumpy, Sleepy and Guilty all in one?) and little fun. It usually does very little for our relationships with our children, since we are probably terribly overcompensating for something or other. We are not doing anything to help the situation, our child's or ourselves.

So let's try to replace Guilt with Genetics! Get mad at your long lost Uncle Herb for being riddled with anxiety. Then forget about it. Move on. And I know great parents with not just one child struggling through life, but two children! Imagine the burden of feeling guilty for this. This, my friends, is another cruel twist of genetics; it's not happening because you had artificial Christmas trees or forgot your child at a birthday party once or twice! It is just what it is. Acceptance is key to truly moving on. Do your best. This will fluctuate from day to day; drop the guilt, try to laugh and, for goodness sake, get out of the house occasionally! See friends, stay fit, share you experiences, seek support and guidance, and try not to take it all too seriously. Worry only when you have to, and then take action, without the cement blocks of guilt around your ankles!

You Can Do It! Actually, You Are Doing It!

In life we often look ahead at some potential obstacle or challenge and think we'll never be able to do it, but, when it's our turn, we get through it! Sometimes we look back and say, "I could never do that again", but actually we could if we had to. We have incredible strength, and often things are not as bad as we may anticipate. So stop anticipating so much. Don't catastrophize the future for you or your child. Take one day at a time; you will both make progress.

I see progress in every child and family I treat, which is why my work is so rewarding. Stay positive and enthusiastic. Be creative about solutions to a challenge. Be realistic about what your child can achieve. By having attainable goals for your children, they will feel more competent, will gain confidence, and maybe even then exceed expectations! There is always more than one way to a destination. Don't get caught in society's sometimes very rigid approach to life. When you have a child who lives outside the box, you need to take a step outside your box of thinking sometimes. There's never just one right way to do something, especially when it comes to children!

Lend a Hand or Two!

If you are now counting your blessings that your child doesn't have a formal psychiatric medical condition, but you know someone who does, reach out. Sometimes the simplest of gestures are very helpful and greatly appreciated. Parenting can be challenging for all of us. Some days we are better than others, so when our good day happens on a friend's bad day, lend a hand; you will likely be rewarded sometime soon.

Points to Remember

Parenting itself is likely one of our biggest challenges. It isn't easy to be attentive, supportive, patient, helpful, insightful, and energetic and fun all the times we need to or want to.

Parenting relatively easy children is challenging enough for most of us!

Parenting children with special needs is nothing short of Heroism! It takes amazing dedication, patience, and insight - stuff money definitely can't buy!

There is hope for ALL children. Nothing stays the same for long!

Guilt is a useless emotion that can encapsulate a parent and render them useless. Find ways to release it!

Remember you are doing your best. Seek guidance and support. Share your experiences and go out with you partner and friends. Personal time is really important!!!

All the other stuff discussed in this book is even more important for families dealing with challenging children. Maybe more difficult, but very important!

Don't forget to Exercise. We need all the extra Stamina we can get!!

Take a drive in your new car!

Chapter Fourteen • Parental Praise

"With the stethoscope of love you listen until you hear the heartbeat of the other."
Barleth and Margaret Hess

Chapter Fourteen
....

Parental Praise
....

Praise or Poison? Be careful what you dish out. Parents are often complimenting children in their efforts and actions in order to encourage them. The thought is that praise will increase self confidence. Sure that is true, but unfortunately, over-praise can lead to inflated self esteem, over-estimation of skill, and can I say it… arrogance! We as parents usually know if we are over-praisers or under-praisers. Both need moderation. Some children need more encouragement than others. As parents we need to know ourselves and our children to see where we stand on this continuum.

Parents are definitely well meaning, but there can be too much of a good thing. Our society is slowly evolving into a very pampered lot, with many children, unfortunately, feeling self entitled. I have seen this in my clinical practice, in society, and in professional settings. It doesn't seem unique to any one group, so what is happening?

Inflated Sense of Entitlement

My theory on this less-than-pleasant attribute of inflated self esteem may well be related to over-praise on mundane issues. There are many things parents should expect from their children respectfully, but appropriately. Children should learn to care for their belongings and environment. They should be taught this with guidance and care, but do they need a wheelbarrow of praise for cleaning their room? Children need encouragement to play sports, an instrument, compete in tournaments, but do they need to be told they are the best, the fastest, the most accomplished when certainly they are not? I do not think so. Actually false praise can have the opposite effect. It may cause complacency or bravado, replacing determination. It can falsely elevate their self expectations and set them up for disappointment. It can make them feel better than others in the wrong kind of way. It can deter them from accepting good guidance - surely not what you were aiming for.

Encouragement and Sensible Praise

Again, being encouraging, keeping things in perspective, and using a bit of humor can help children see themselves accurately and help them truly appreciate their many strengths and fewer areas of need. They will be better able to self-evaluate and seek assistance when necessary and offer help when able!

As parents, the objective should be to try to raise a child who is able to balance strong self worth with the courage to be kind and the confidence to be tolerant! In my experience, it is the grounded child, confident in who they are, who can be at ease with kindness to others and allow others their individuality. To actually enjoy others' diversity and individuality can bring great joys and diversity into one's own life. Help your child see value in others, value in the spectrum of life. Different means opportunity, not inferiority. Adolescents who are narrower-minded are at risk of missing out on many exciting opportunities. An open mind will embrace change, differences, and tolerance. It will allow them to learn from others, which will certainly enrich their lives.

Children certainly do need recognition for effort, especially in something they have been struggling with and have found some success. Acknowledging effort is more effective than just commenting on the result. For example, praise about success on a test result could sound like this: "I am proud of you for working so hard and really finding a way to be successful in this course, how do you feel about how you did?". Acknowledging effort helps your child see the link between effort and reward. If your child is being critical about a team member not playing well, remind your child that everyone has good and bad days and that effort, again, is what counts, for example: "I know you feel frustrated about his playing tonight, but you know everyone has good and bad days. It looked to me that he was working hard, and maybe something was going on with him we aren't aware of. Perhaps you should give him a break and recognize his effort." When children are good at getting their chores done, like keeping a tidy room, helping out with dishes, feeding the dog, it is helpful to identify their contribution, like this maybe: "You're doing well with your chores, it really helps me when you contribute like this and take care of your space. I think it is really important that you learn to help around the house, because this is your house too. Learning how to take care of your things will help you become more independent. Also, when we get through the clean up early, it leaves us more time for fun, so what would you like to do together now as our reward for good team work?".

Expressing gratitude and how well your children are contributing to the family unit is important; tying in the gratitude with a natural consequence of the behaviour is a way of hitting home the message of cause and effect. You help out and we get to do good things. A simple equation. They don't need $20 to make a bed; they just need to learn that team work pays off with team benefits and personal growth. Recognizing personal growth is also important. So when

Chapter Fifteen • Adjusting Our Parenting Approach on an As-Needed Basis!!

your son or daughter has their first babysitting gig, something like this may sound nice: "I am really proud of how you handled this first job! You were really mature about it and I am impressed with your dedication to learning what you needed to, to be a reliable and successful babysitter. Well done!" Our children go from being looked after to looking after others, very, very quickly.

Points to remember

Keep praise appropriate and genuine.

Support is important, but inflated praise can lead to inflated self worth!

Help your child develop self worth that is strong enough to embrace kindness and tolerance of others. Balance, as always, is key!

"Say 'well done' when things are done well."
Fr.JJM

Chapter Fifteen

Adjusting Our Parenting Approach, on an As-Needed Basis!!

Children change every day. Their cognitive capabilities evolve, they see things differently, and they experience the world differently every day. As children change, so must parents. The trick is keeping up with them!

Bend a Little

Let's start with the concept of Flexibility, a concept full of wisdom! As parents, we are often asking, even demanding, that our children be able to go with the flow. Oops, another change in the routine, come on, hurry up, let's go…yada yada yada! And yes, it is a great trait to be able to switch gears, drop everything, and go at a moment's notice, change tracks and leave the mess behind you - you get the picture! We need to be able to move on, go sideways, and reverse whenever necessary. It makes living in a busy and exciting world a lot easier if we can do that, and it is important to help your children learn this. By being flexible yourself, by

Chapter Fifteen • Adjusting Our Parenting Approach on an As-Needed Basis!!

being able to switch gears easily, let go of unfinished business for a while for a greater cause, and not get too frazzled, your children will see this, and most of them will adopt the same approach. It's not the same as being a chronic non-completer, a scatter-brain, or being disorganized. It simply means you can redirect your focus when necessary and not be too worried about it. If this doesn't come easily to you and you are somewhat inflexible, then likely your children will also adopt that approach!

So take a look at your style and try working on it if it needs a little tweaking. Discuss it with your partner and/or children and come up with some plans to try to become more spontaneous! Like the fire drills at school, you don't have to inform everyone a drill is coming, but they will be aware that the drill is important. Be spontaneous with yourself, drop everything [except the baby!] one evening, and go to a movie, take a walk, or go to the grocery store. A change can be as good as a rest!

Just as our children need flexibility to better field life's curve balls, and we need to be able to dodge spit balls with agility, our parenting approach also needs some built in flexibility. All children and adults proceed through life by attaining various developmental stages. There are a number of theories about development, but the basic premise is that we should master one stage before we can move on successfully to the next stage.

It's not so important that you memorize these stages, but that you appreciate the fact that children have their work cut out for them! So they need us, as parents, to be able to adapt to their needs through these various stages. Most of us have our preferred parenting approach: some of us are more disciplinarian, some are very passive, some are very protective, and the variations go on and on. Put two people together in a marriage, and the parenting style combo possibilities go wild! Sometimes we complement each other, sometimes we don't! So there are two issues: how we approach our children and how we work with our partners on approaching our children!

Self Awareness

Let's start with the issue of how we can become a little fluid with our kids. First, recognize where you lie on the firm to soft scale. Take a look at how you approach their resistance, opposition, and possible aggression. How do you do when they are anxious? Do you get anxious? Self-reflection will help you see how you are most of the time and enable you to see if that point of reference is always the most appropriate. Ask your partner what they think your style is and try to not be too defensive! For example, if you know that you get quite anxious when your child pleads to you not to go out to your exercise class, and you concede to stay home, maybe you need to adjust your approach! If you are very passive and non-confrontational, and your toddler was soo good, but changed into a very oppositional 11 year-old trying to find their place in their peer world, maybe you need to be more firm and help them with limit-setting better.

If we find ourselves too rigid in discipline and routine, we may find ourselves in many a battle with an oppositional child. Our children are trying to master their worlds, but they need our kind, patient, but maybe also firm direction at times. The demands on them are many; society offers them many choices and temptations, and they need our help in navigating through it all. What may have worked for us in getting our child toilet trained, may not be the most effective when dealing with marijuana use. Take stock of what your parenting style is, be aware that your children are working hard in mastering their developmental challenges, and, as they mature and experience the world, we will likely need to wear many different parenting hats. Going against the grain of our own personal style can be really difficult, but could save you and your child a lot of grief!

The Mirror Effect

An example of this is the rather anxious, quite watchful parent, who probably has some real anxiety themselves, which increases when having to deal with an anxious child. What that child needs is for their parent/s to be relaxed, confident, encouraging, and firm with them when they are panicking. The child needs to be able to express their anxiety but be confident in their parent's encouragement and, sometimes, insistence. For example, if the child is crying at the classroom threshold, not wanting to separate from Mom or Dad, the parent needs to be kind but firm in their insistence that the child go to class. It goes against every grain in us as parents to leave our child upset, let alone crying, but it may be exactly what they need! It takes any parent great strength to do that, let alone a parent who themselves is anxious and feeling very similar to their child. Talk about digging deep! It's like standing up straight against a huge wave! Going against our own tide can be extremely challenging, but frequently necessary in the life of a parent.

It is my clinical experience when working with teens and their parents about communication, relationship issues, and general "getting along" issues, that the teen and I usually share the same opinion of the parental issues. As parents, our parenting and communication style is usually pretty consistent and often not easy to accurately self- assess. Our children, however, can usually sum us up quite precisely!! I usually ask teens or children what they would like their parents to do differently and the same for the parent - what would they like their kids to do differently. This is an easy thing to do at home, either as a group discussion or one-on-one. Keep in mind not to be too defensive. If we can't take feedback from our kids, who can we listen to! After you get through the allowance and curfew issues, dig a little deeper. Our children are very insightful, and their input can be invaluable. They are not trying to be hurtful, just honest.

Bending with Grown-up!

Now, getting along with the grown-ups in the house - that's a bit tougher! We all come from varying backgrounds and parenting experiences of our own. So not only do our children have to deal with one captain, they have to deal with two captains, who may be frequently at odds about how to and where to steer the ship. One captain may be away for weeks at a time working and then be home for weeks at a time watching their every move. Maybe they live with one parent and their grandparents - wow, a generation gap as well as three captains! You get the picture. There are lots of variations on the theme, or decision, or when to come in on a Friday night. So it may be Very Good time spent if the captains had regular discussions on how to navigate.

I see a lot of grief come out of situations where parents are on opposite poles. When parental approaches are so different, children may act very differently with either parent, or the presence of one parent can sabotage the efforts of the other. This can lead to lots of confusion for children and lots of discord for parents. For example, problems can arise if one parent is very lenient, doesn't follow through with discipline and allows disrespect, while the other parent feels cooperation, respect, and limit-setting is important. Each parent can feel that the other is wrong, and each

Chapter Fifteen • Adjusting Our Parenting Approach on an As-Needed Basis!!

parent can feel alienated, let alone the children! Communication and compromise is really important in parenting to avoid bigger problems. It's one thing to disagree about bedtime, but it is more difficult and damaging to all parties involved when one parent has zero tolerance on drug and alcohol use while the other parent is much more lenient.

Whatever your personal style, as a two-parent family (or some other variation of the theme) you need to reach a consensus, which is usually a compromise, on important issues and try to stand united. Talk about which approach would be most beneficial for your child. Ordinarily when we discuss something, we realize that we are not that far apart and usually have the same goal in mind. Practising this is important. Talk, talk, talk! It helps, helps, helps!!

Alien Invasion

Another big time of adjustment for everyone is usually around teen time! When you find yourself wondering, "Who are you and what did you do with my daughter??" It may be that Estrogen has silently slipped in and replaced her with someone who looks like your daughter, occasionally sounds like your daughter, but has a definite dramatic, moody, snappy, self-righteous, sensitive edge! Even with the most loving of children, girls and boys too, adolescent hormones can bring quite a jolt to everyone in the family! If you find your tension rising, remind yourself that this too is okay. It does demand a flexible approach, a big infusion of patience, and even more communication. It can be very challenging and make a parent feel alienated when their little darling is now fiercely independent, more reclusive, and really not much interested in you. It is very important to not take this transitional behaviour personally. Young teens are moving through a normal phase to independence, which is really what good parenting is working towards: happy, interpersonal, successful, and independent people! So this passage of adolescence, while painful for many, is a necessary evil!

Connecting with Aliens!

So how do you stay connected to your young teen during this phase without a lot of conflict and tension, while remaining a responsible and caring parent? Patience is key, and reminding yourself that although your teen may be pushing you away, it's the time they likely need you the most. With so many opposing influences in their lives, they need your calm, steady guidance. They need to be with you. It may be difficult scheduling yourself into their schedule, competing with friends, friends and more friends, sleep, and hopefully school, other activities, and on and on it goes. You must not take 'no' for an answer and slot yourself in. You may need to be creative, accommodating, and very persistent, but the time you spend together doing positive things will make it a lot easier and even possible to be the one they go to for guidance, questions, and support. Find a common interest. You may need to create a common interest - it likely wouldn't be the first time you developed an interest in something for a person of interest! There is no substitute for spending time together. Even if you find your budding or full-blown teen a little hard to take, remember you are mainly responsible for who has developed right in front of you. And also remember that nothing stays the same for long!

It is essential that you remain the parent; your teen needs guidance, rules, and discipline. They also need to be heard and respected. By being respectful to your teen, you model the behaviour you

Chapter Fifteen • Adjusting Our Parenting Approach on an As-Needed Basis!!

expect back. Regardless of most circumstances, respect should be expected by you from your teen. Address issues of disrespect early, because bad habits can form fast and easy. Be respectful on your addressing of the issue, and model what you expect. Be patient and present. It will pay off, and soon enough your teen will evolve into someone you really like spending time with and will likely remind you of someone you know!

The Road to Independence (Long and Winding)

It can be an emotional sting that can really hurt when your once adoring child, in the sense of adoring you, now is more independent, and all at once you are more needy of them! As parents, the goal is to help your child develop independence; the lack of this developmental skill is pretty problematic. But still, when it starts to happen, parents can feel a little at a loss. It takes some readjusting, looking at the relationship a little differently, and being proud of both of you that this is actually happening!

Now your child still needs you immensely, but just in somewhat different ways. Your approach to supervision will need to change; now you need to learn how to stay up later and either watch some TV with them, drive them to places, drive them to places and drive them to places, then pick them up, which is really important, and be up when they get home, at a reasonable time of course! Being awake, coherent, not at the bottom end of a litre of wine is really, really important! By being there when they get home or by picking them up, they know you have a better sense of the situation. Curfew is more respected, and how they arrive to your presence is more of an issue. If teens are drinking, for example, and you are picking them up, or home waiting to have a conversation with them, they will likely try to be in good shape when they see you.

This may translate in drinking half as much, which is a good thing! Anything you can do to instill responsibility and making good decisions is very crucial at this stage. They need to know you are on top of things, and this issue of being present at midnight really does make a difference.

The way you give advice now may need to be more subtle, more discreet. Parenting now needs a bit more savvy. Your presence, while now a little more elusive, is even more important. That is important to remember. Don't count yourself out, just a little to the left! But, boy oh boy, that position is ultra important! Teens still want parental input and guidance. There are still many uncertainties for them to cope with, and they will need you.

Points to Remember

Our children's needs change as they progress through their developmental stages. Their ability to understand different concepts will change with maturing cognition.

Our parenting style can be a little fixed, so what may have worked for us with our younger child may not be what they need as they progress!

Be open to adjusting your approach; your children need you to do that to ensure that they get the guidance they need.

Talk to your children and partner. They may have insights that you can't easily see, or they may help you understand the impact of your parenting style. It is so much easier for others to see certain things about us!!

Chapter Fifteen • Adjusting Our Parenting Approach on an As-Needed Basis!!

Try to be on the same chapter as your partner, if not the same page! A united approach will go further in getting the results you want and mean less nights sleeping on the couch!

The teen years are challenging, but also another great opportunity to bond with your child! Be patient and present.

Flexibility is good for all of us!

Did I mention driving can be fun! Maybe a new car would help!

"A spoonful of sugar helps the medicine go down."
Robert and Richard Sherman

Chapter Sixteen
....

If You Could See Me Now!! Self evolution is inevitable, thank goodness!
....

This chapter was inspired by the shocking sight of me sitting at my desk one day. It is only recently that I came kicking and screaming into the world of technology. I still prefer the paper copy, the face-to-face or voice-to-voice conversations, and actually going to the bank! Some of this entrenchment in traditional interactions is based on interpersonal preferences, some on my background or ERA, and some on lack of skill set and the limitation of time and motivation to learn it.

So one day very recently as I was sitting at my desk, I noted with surprise and amazement that I had made some progress in the IT world and maybe had even turned the corner. I was using Skype on my laptop, while checking my documents on my other computer, and I had just laid down my new Blackberry Storm which I was using to find something on my email. I had three computers on at once and was actually using them! Now this doesn't happen often, nor should it, but the sheer fact that it happened at all brought me to the thought of self evolution. I thought if I could get to this point with IT usage, well anyone could do anything! Self evolution usually happens despite our traditions, reluctance, or fears. So embrace it, nudge it along, play with it, and enjoy it!

Parental Growth

Parenting is an evolution. We begin with many expectations for our children and ourselves as parents. We progress through physical exhaustion while parenting our babies, then after a few years of "wow this is really easy now", we flow into parenting the teen years and experience mental exhaustion. We evolve as the needs of our children change. We need to adapt to their varying developmental stages, their personality formation, and their cognitive capabilities.

Let's look at discipline, defiance, and parental tolerance. Maybe our child has become more defiant, or their defiance hasn't changed but their behaviour is just age-appropriate and leads to more serious issues. If we have been rather laid back in the discipline area, non-confrontational, well maybe it's time to strengthen the parental backbone. This is not easy to do, but necessary. Disciplinary tactics which worked for younger children may need to be tweaked to handle the newly autonomous teen.

Maybe our child has been dealing with anxiety and shyness for many years, but started making progress and is now becoming more independent. This would make most of us both happy and uneasy at the same time. As a parent, you know that your child has to become more independent and social as this will help her confidence. But it is hard to let go. You feel scared for her, you're not used to her going without you, and you don't want her to get hurt or anxious. You have spent most of the time protecting and helping her, but now you have to let her go - not far, just the movie, but it feels like China! But you can do it and you will, if you have to. We can change as parents, and often we have to in order to meet the needs of our children. Flexibility is something we should be teaching our children, and ourselves every day.

Personal Growth

Evolving as a parent is a big part of self evolution, but how about evolving as a person. We have so many stages in development, and they don't stop when we become parents. As we start off parenting young children, we are somewhat novice in most areas. Learning how to get out of the house within two hours with small kids, even one, can be extremely challenging. How to navigate through temper tantrums, theirs and yours, and how to swing through a week-long birthday celebration for your three year-old is another stage! We learn as we go. Our experience grows, as does our confidence. Our children progress, meet challenges, and we get through them together.

So as you emerge from the parenting trenches, start looking within yourself more with respect to what you want out of life for you and your children. Pause regularly to take note of where you all are. Have you met some of your earlier objectives? Have you been the parent you intended to be? Are there things about yourself you want to change? This process takes reflection and time. Writing things down can be very powerful. It's like balancing your chequing account - sometimes until we see it in black and white, we don't take it seriously.

Taking your personal inventory can also be more effective when you see things in writing. List your accomplishments. It may surprise you just how well you have done. Don't dismiss what you have achieved. Note what you had to do to get where you are, and then write down where you want to go from here. Make a map of how you can get there. Look at your personal growth wish list and prioritize the objectives you have set. Be realistic, but also positive and optimistic. This is your list, for your eyes only. On the map, add in what you need to do along the way. Put this document of self-growth somewhere where you can keep it private if need be, but accessible so you can review it regularly. We often set financial goals, so why not self-improvement goals.

We need to pay attention to ourselves in a positive way in order to stay self-fulfilled and interested in our lives. There is so much in life to explore, but it is very easy to become complacent. Routine can be comforting and necessary, but if never broken, very encapsulating. We can get lost in the ease of it all. We need routine to a degree - stability is important to us and our families - but not complacency. Don't settle for just 'getting along'. Life can be so much better for you and your family when you self-monitor. Make sure the road you're on is the one intended, not an easy shortcut. It is the journey that matters, the day-to-day, because today is really all any of us have. So enjoy it, make it count.

Your Child's Map

It is also very helpful to review your expectations for your children. The first step is to recognize who they truly are. What are their personality traits? What are their strengths and needs? Remember back to previous expectations. Are they changed, and have you been able to help them achieve what you intended, what they intended? Ask your children what their expectations are. Again, writing things down can have tremendous impact. Having things in writing make them more real. Like making a promise out loud, it has witness and now cannot be ignored.

Make a map together with your child. It must be age-appropriate; it can be simple or elaborate. Get them to be very active in it, using illustrations, color, powerful and empowering statements. This can help them develop their own sense of self, their own goals and ambitions. Revisit it regularly, make modifications and show them that there is more than one route to a goal. Help them see that goals can change, flexibility is good, priorities change. We are always evolving, and this process can help them see this without self criticism. Not many things stay the same in life for long, and seeing this can help us through tough times, to see that life is fluid helps us and our children learn how to roll with the waves. The tide changes, and, while our goals may remain similar, there are many routes to success.

By leading by example in our own personal growth and by taking inventory of our goals for our children and ourselves, we show and bring our children to a place of ease in their own journey to self discovery. By attempting to reach our own potential in a flexible, caring way, we show how healthy and important this is. When we recognize our strengths, the meaning of true self confidence, our potential soars. With motivation to be our best, we can be our best parenting self and our best personal self. Be patient with yourself and your children, supportive and respectful of each other, and incredible things will happen. That saying, "All in good time," is quite wise. With perseverance, support, and using our strengths, we will succeed at our goals. Having goals is an essential step - they initially may be vague or broad, but we all need to have them. And we all have the capability to achieve them. Be your own leader and your child's. You just may surprise yourself!

Being active in looking at how and where your lives are going (yours and your child's) may mean cutting back on activities. As a society, we are very driven to perform. Many parents

Chapter Sixteen • If You Could See Me Now!

complain how exhausted they are bringing their children to all their activities - imagine how the child feels! Children are often expected to punch in adult days. Parents are afraid to let their child miss out on a practice, a lesson, a tournament, just in case their child falls behind. We interject such competitiveness and urgency into these events! The child is fine to miss it usually, but then the parent points out how much they may fall behind and miss out, not be as good as the other child, not make the team, not be first, blah blah blah. Very confidence-bursting motivation! Are we so wrapped up in the success of it all that the fun is lost? Whose life is it anyway?

Parents must absolutely direct, encourage, and sometimes push a little. As discussed earlier, being involved in structured activities is important, but we must always use good, sound, common sense. Look at the balance: is there time for play, family time, personal down time? Be careful: don't overload your child, be mindful of balance. Guard against getting caught up in the societal craziness of 'doing it all'. Children can get 'burned out' too. If a child feels they cannot keep up with parental expectations for recreation events, how demoralizing is that! Children can become way too driven to perfection; they no longer then do the activity for the mere pleasure of it, but to attain something. A spot in the symphony displaces the love of flute, an NHL draft is the driving force for the novice hockey player, the dance class must lead to the Canadian Ballet, and so on. Instead of just enjoying the fun, some children are driven to search for perfection. That drive to perfection can be via a very bumpy, lonely, and disappointing road. The road to dance class with a detour to ice cream, though, is a little more fun! Make sure your child doesn't pay the price for living, or trying to live, your dream. Everyone can dream, but everyone has their own dream.

I see many children in my practice stressed out due to their very ambitious activity level. Most of these children are strongly internally driven; they want to do well for themselves; and they feel an intense need to be 'Top in the Class' in order to feel fulfilled. They drive themselves very hard and usually don't feel satisfied with great results unless they are top results. Unless a child has significant difficulty with motivation, and I know very few of these types of children, they want to succeed. Children want to do well, be accepted, and please their parents. When parents don't recognize this and push their child too hard, the child has great risk of not being able to correctly self-evaluate. That's because they are not responding to what they think is reasonable any longer, but to what their parent thinks is good enough. And if that 'good enough' is not attainable for that child, then they could get programmed to always be looking for something in themselves that is not there, and not appreciate what they can do and who they really are. So be careful what you wish for: pushing your child into an overachieving, self-deprecating individual is probably not what you were aiming for! Appropriate self appreciation and self evaluation is the basis of self esteem. Helping your child reach their potential in a supportive, sometimes directive manner, while acknowledging their strengths and needs, will lead to a balanced sense of self.

Points to Remember

Everyone evolves, makes progress, changes, adapts. Monitoring self evolution is helpful: are you going in the right direction, at the right pace, with the right people?

It's important to self reflect on our personal life plan and self expectations.

Writing down goals is powerful. Use a map to see the route, the journey.

Reflect with your children on what they want out of life, help them with their own map. Visualization can be very powerful for children. This process can help children feel empowered that they have choices; they can see that individuals are the masters of their own destiny!

Our dreams are not necessarily our children's dreams! Allowing a child to be an individual can be challenging, but is essential. Children need parents to help them feel confident in their own abilities, to succeed at what they want. Parental direction is important, appropriate encouragement essential, but balanced with tolerance and acceptance.

Balance is very important. Society is increasingly urging children to take on enormous activity loads. Trust your judgment. Be sensible about extra-curricular activities.

"If you ask for wisdom, you will get common sense."
Fr. JJM

Chapter Seventeen

Words from the Peanut Gallery

In my clinical practice, I often ask children what they like about themselves, their parents and families, what they would like to see change in their family members and themselves for relationships to improve or deepen. Even families with great things going on, which are most families, can use some tweaking! Relationships are a fluid thing; they are always changing because people are always changing. Life is not static, stressors fluctuate, our ability to navigate life changes, our priorities shift. That's part of life.

Invariably parents are a little surprised with what their children reveal! Often children offer very insightful comments, those parents find helpful. Usually we just haven't asked our children these questions; sometimes we are a little apprehensive about what they may say and don't feel prepared or capable of meeting their expectations. It has been my experience in my clinical practice that the comments that are shared are usually very helpful and very attainable - sometimes with a little work - but attainable. It opens up the communication about what our children see as important and what can be done about their concerns or wishes, as well as opening up a parent's mind to their child's. Perception is reality in many cases, especially in a child's mind. So this kind of open communication can help a parent understand their child's

Chapter Seventeen • Words from the Peanut Gallery.....

perspective and discuss it. Parents cannot fulfill all wishes, but wishes can be discussed, put in perspective, and better understood. When a child feels listened to, just like adults, they feel better valued and understood. Important feelings indeed!

I thought some Child Perspectives may provide some nice examples of how some children see their worlds! My own children, as well as some of their friends, have offered to share some insights. So, from the mouths of Babes!!

What do you like about your parents?

A: When they do fun stuff with me, when we spend time together, like on rainy days, we watch a movie. Calm, when they don't get mad at me. *9 years*
A: When we do fun things like build a rink, go on holidays, go to the movies. When they are calm and kind. *10 yrs*
A: They are kind, they help me out, and they are generous! *10 years*
A: They take care of me, and they are really kind and generous and always doing stuff like keeping the house okay and keeping me safe. *10 years*
A: They are really understanding of what I do and help me with my problems, I can confide in them. *12 years*
A: They let me have friends over. They let me play my Wii and DS. *6 years*
A: They're very funny. *8 years*
A: They are kind and understanding of what problems I might have. *11 years*
A: What I like about my parents is that they give me support and they are always there for me. They like me for who I am. *13 years*

A: What I like about my parents, they love me and take of me. *11 years*
A: I like that they provide for me, and let me do fun things. *13 years*
A: They provide me with shelter and food. *16 years*

What do you like doing with your family?

A: Going for walks and going to new or old places together. *10 years*
A: Going out to restaurants, eating together at home, seeing movies, and going on trips. *10 years*
A: I like going on trips together, movies and having movie night at home, and playing board games. *12 years*
A: I like playing with my family. I like family game night with my family. *6 years*
A: I like playing sports with my Dad and going shopping with my Mom and my Dad. *8 years*
A: I like to go outside and be active together. I like going places with them. I like doing things that my parents and brothers like and doing things that I like. *11 years*
A: I just like spending quality time with my family. *13 years*
A: What I like doing with my family is going on vacation and just having every day fun. *11 years*
A: I like having family dinners. *13 years*
A: I like to watch movies, play games. *16 years*

What makes a family work well, makes things good?

A: When we are not grumpy, when we get sleep! *10 years*
A: When we all love each other and get along. *10 years*

Chapter Seventeen • Words from the Peanut Gallery.....

A: A combination of helping each other and sharing workload in the house and just being nice to each other and being respectful. *12 years*
A: When we work as a team, and whenever there is hard times we all help out. *13 years*
A: Sharing workload in the house and just being nice to each other and being respectful. *12 years*
A: Being nice and loving each other. *6 years*
A: Loving and sharing. *8 years*
A: Understanding each other. Getting along well. *11 years*
A: When we work as a team and whenever there are hard times we all help out. *13 years*
A: What makes things go smoothly is when we all pitch in and do our daily chores. *11 years*
A: My mom! *13 years*
A: Talking to each other, joking around *16 years*

What is your wish list for your family?

A: To go on trips and do special things like going to hockey games, soccer games. *10 years*
A: Don't argue as much. *10 years*
A: We would go to a lot of tropical places with each other. *12 years*
A: Play with toys together and play games. *6 years*
A: I'd like to go on some trips like to Florida and do things together as a family. *8 years*
A: That we'll always have a great time together. Sometimes we might argue but we'll always work our way through it. Go on trips together so we can be together a lot. *11 years*
A: That we stay together and continue to support one another with love. *13 years*

A: My wish for my family would be that my Daddy would come back to life because we all miss him and love him very much. *11 years*
A: A few more vacations. *13 years*
A: That we stay the way we are. *16 years*

So you can see, children see our kindness and love, and appreciate these qualities. Children want to spend time together as a family and have fun together. They remember fun times and want more of them. Ask your children these same questions and see where they lead you. You may be surprised, you may learn something, or you may just be reassured. Whatever you discover, likely you will go and do something fun together, real soon!

Listening is very important. First you must ask.

"To give is a joy; to receive is a pleasure; to share is a virtue."
Fr. JJM

Gratitude

Our lives with our children and partners are a journey. There is no perfection, just effort and evolution. Our relationships begin with expectations, and we grow together with awareness. We journey together through lots of good, some not so good, and even some rough times. Don't let false expectations about relationships fool you into thinking that your relationships are not great or wonderful. There is a lot of false advertisement out there that sometimes make us feel that as parents we are not making the grade, that we are not doing it right. People put their best outwards, so what we see is often just a glimpse of reality, not the whole of it. Sure, that outward display may very well be sincere and true, but every relationship and family has its ups and downs, its highs and lows. That is life. And life is for experiencing and sharing.

As families we are exposed to much family media, sitcoms, reality shows, movies, novels - lots of family images. But the only family image that really matters is your family image, its imprint. It's like fingerprints: no-one else's are the same. We are all different individuals making up our families, so why wouldn't each family be different?

It is so okay to get exhausted parenting your children. It means you are trying. It is very fine to get disappointed that your partner..... well anything. It means you care if you guys get it right together. If you react, it means you care, you are engaged.

Nothing stays the same for long. The sheer passage of time changes most things, let alone effort, love, and attention. Being aware of your relationships with your family, nurturing them and also very importantly taking care of yourself are vital components to successful relationships. There is no one right way to do it. Be healthy, happy, and balanced.

Enjoy your journey, be patient to you and yours. Allow yourself to be in the moment. The greatest moment of your life is always now! Give thanks for your gifts, appreciate your blessings, and have fun.

A very special thank-you to my "Reading Group". Many friends and family agreed to read this book for me for suggestions and comments. Many of us met to discuss their opinion of the book, and this process was extremely helpful! So thank you Dad, Suzanne, John, Donna and Catherine, Christine S, Pamela H, Barbara D, Karen B, Susan D, Christine D, Mary W, Lisa H, Stephanie T, Eileen O, Christine M, Stacey H, Michelle W, Annette W, Lorraine P, Victoria C, Millie and Dave B...... and Sharon Burry, who has been so helpful and wonderful throughout this whole process!!! And Father John, thank you so much for your inspiring quotes and support! Your insights, as always, are truly invigorating! I am blessed to have you in my life.

During our 'Readers Group', I found we had a great discussion about parenting in general, and we all learned from each other. Collaborating with friends about parenting can be very helpful and encouraging. Perhaps your own 'reading group' around this book may provide you and some friends an opportunity to share ideas and be a support for each other. We also had food, which can be fun too!

Kristann, you are amazing, patient, and very kind! As well as a fabulous editor you have been a great support! Many, many thanks!!

Leigh-Ann, thank you for your creativity, enthusiasm and patience!

Susan Drodge, your keen eye and unassuming grace have been a gift granted!

Thank-you to Robert & Lynn Young from Celebrity Photo Studio for their expertise & generosity

Thanks, Dad, for everything!

Thank you to my wonderful family, and thank you Monika and Timothy, my beautiful children, for being you.

Thank you to my patients and families, and thank you for reading this! Happy parenting :)

Sincerely,

Barbara Maddigan, M.D., FRCPC

"There is nothing better than the encouragement of a good friend."
Katherine Butler Hathaway

Barbara Maddigan
M.D., FRCPC

....

I was born in Montreal, the youngest of five children, and the daughter of two wonderful parents, both Newfoundlanders. Life was great and then at the age of 12, my parents, one sister, and I moved to New Brunswick, and then six months later to Newfoundland! I was very fortunate to see lots of our great country and meet so many wonderful people along the way.

I went to Memorial University of Newfoundland and Labrador, or MUN, where I received a Bachelor's of Science in Biochemistry, and then my Medical Degree. I went on to complete a residency in Psychiatry and sub specialized in Child and Adolescent Psychiatry. I had amazing teachers and mentors. I was fortunate enough to do a three-month elective during my psychiatry training in Ottawa at the Children's Hospital of Eastern Ontario. Here, again, I met some amazing people, and was supervised by very skilled and caring physicians/psychiatrists.

I started my clinical career at the Janeway Children's Hospital in St. John's, Newfoundland in 1995. I was an Assistant Professor at Memorial University of Newfoundland, the Psychiatry Training Program's curriculum director for a couple of years and then became the Director of Training for the Psychiatry Training Program. I was promoted to Associate Professor at Memorial University in 2004, and then after my six-year term as the Psychiatry Residency Training Program Director, I decided to leave hospital based practice and went into community practice. I had to leave a salaried position with the Hospital as well as with the University, to which I had been connected for a long time. I made this somewhat risky move in order to spend more time with my children while they were still young.

That was six years ago, and it was one of the best decisions I have ever made! Now that they are a little older, my time with them is even more precious. I still have a very active and busy medical practice and a very busy and fulfilling life with my wonderful family. I was so fortunate to be in the position to 'think outside the box' career wise, and I thank God I took the chance. Adding more balance and autonomy to my life has only enhanced my clinical work, and after 15years of practice I still look forward to seeing my patients! My own children and my patients continue to teach me every day. Thank you all.

Phew, writing the book was easy; now deciding what's for supper, that's challenging!
B. Maddigan!

Notes: